MEN:
SOME ASSEMBLY REQUIRED

Chuck Snyder

PUBLISHING
Colorado Springs, Colorado

MEN: SOME ASSEMBLY REQUIRED
Copyright © 1995 by Chuck Snyder. All rights reserved. International copyright secured.

Library of Congress Cataloging-in-Publication Data
Snyder, Chuck.
    Men: some assembly required: a woman's guide to understanding a man / Chuck Snyder.
        p. cm.
    Includes bibliographical references.
    ISBN 1-56179-344-2
    1. Men—Psychology.   2. Women—Attitudes.   3.   Man—woman relationships.
I. Title.
HQ1090.S65   1995
646.7'0081—dc20
                                                    95-1538
                                                     CIP

Published by Focus on the Family Publishing, Colorado Springs, CO 80995. Distributed in the U. S. A. and Canada by Word Books, Dallas, Texas.

Unless otherwise noted, Scripture quotations are from *The Living Bible*,© 1971. Used by permission of Tyndale House Publishers, Inc., Wheaton, IL 60189. All rights reserved.

Editor: Gwen Weising
Front cover design: Avrea Foster
Illustration: Benjamin Vincent

Printed in the United States of America
  96 97 98 99/10 9 8 7 6 5 4 3

This book is dedicated to the people most responsible for teaching me how a woman thinks:

Mrs. Barb Snyder
Dr. James Dobson
Gary Smalley
Mrs. Kay Arthur

I will be eternally grateful.

Special thanks to the hundreds of women and men who were kind enough to help with this project by participating in my surveys, and to Gwen Ellis, my editor. Her wisdom and writing skills added so much. I'm thankful for her tender, loving care.

I'm honored to have been on God's team as Chuck's "third party" to help him understand how Barb was designed. Now maybe he can help you better understand a man.

> Gary Smalley
> President / Founder of Today's Family

We have known and appreciated Chuck and Barb Snyder for many years. The readers of this book will find it humorous as it offers insights into how a man's mind works. As husband and wife of 37 years, we were reminded how really funny it is when we think differently.

> Larry and Judy Burkett
> Christian Financial Concepts

You think your husband is missing a few parts . . . maybe has a couple of emotional bolts loose? Don't panic and don't give up! Help is in your hands.

Men: Some Assembly Required *is the wit and wisdom of a gentle saint from Seattle. Chuck Snyder offers proven advice seasoned with grace—a set of blueprints for building enduring love in marriages that want to stand the test of time.*

> Tim Kimmel
> Author of *Powerful Personalities*

When Chuck Snyder talks . . . I listen! That's because his message is always life-lifting and life-changing—just like the message of Men: Some Assembly Required.

> John Trent, Ph. D.
> Author of *Life Mapping*
> President of Encouraging Words

Contents

Foreword

This is "vintage" Chuck, and if you have ever heard Chuck or Barb Snyder speak on the subject of marriage or the horrendous adjustment of understanding and living with a mate that just isn't like you, then you know that "vintage" Chuck is good stuff.

It's folksy—just plain folks and down-to-earth where you can relate. Easy to read!

It's humorous—which always helps the medicine go down in a most delightful way.

It's insightful—you'll gain valuable insights into that man you're married to.

It's medicinal—good medicine for what ails your understanding and appreciation of your mate.

It's encouraging—isn't it always encouraging to find out you're not alone?

Men do require some assembly, but once that happens and you get them assembled, you've got a good thing going. You'll have a marriage that can mirror for the world the relationship of Jesus Christ and His bride: taught in Ephesians 5. The world needs to see marriages like this—marriages that are going to last as long as each of the partners is around because both are unconditionally committed, first of all, to God and, second, to each other.

Chuck's book will help. That's why he wrote it. He wants to serve you by sharing what God has taught him and, in turn taught, so effectively through him and Barb.

And you know what? Chuck and Barb are as real and as genuine as they sound. Jack and I know. We've lived with them and been blessed and ministered to by them.

Kay Arthur
Executive Vice President
Precept Ministries

A Word from Chuck

I would like to start this book by honoring my precious wife, Barb, and her contribution to this work. She has been so patient during my construction. I'm not fully assembled yet, but she supports me as God uses my mistakes as learning tools for others going through the same problems I've experienced.

Barb's teaching gift has enriched and brought God's light to many of the concepts I talk about. Her wisdom edited out some parts of this manuscript that might have offended. Her tolerance allowed me to leave in some parts that might offend but that might also help people more closely honor biblical principles. Her sense of humor has allowed me to include some stories that she would probably tell differently. Her undying loyalty has kept me close to home. Her gifts of children and grandchildren have brought so much sunshine and laughter to my life. I'll always appreciate her many sacrifices, including giving me a puppy to train on the rug.

How do I love Barb? In countless ways. She's the reason I can write this extended letter to you. She has been the key player on God's team as He has taught me all the things I need to know to help you. If I'm ever able to sit in the gates with the elders, it will be because of what she has done and Whose she is. If I ever receive honor in this world, I'll defer it all to her. She was God's starting point for my assembly, and she has my deepest gratitude for eternity.

I have two purposes for this book. One is to help you understand how a man's mind works. Did you know that he doesn't mean to be insensitive or one-dimensional? Can you believe that he doesn't make you miserable on purpose? He really does care. He's just ignorant about the ways of a woman. No one has ever taught him about the differences between men and women. By the time you finish reading this book you'll have a clearer understanding of how a man is designed.

The second purpose for this book may be even more important to me. I want to make you laugh. Now, that doesn't sound like a very lofty goal for a book, does it? But in my opinion you as a woman have to carry more than your share of the burdens of the world, and life for you may not seem to be very much fun. Often your burdens are increased by having a man in your life. Believe me when I say that he really doesn't mean to be uncaring and not meet your needs. He just has never been taught. I know this causes you sorrow, but I hope I can help you look at the man in your life and laugh a little bit.

I have two challenges in writing this book. My first is to convince you I know something about what a woman needs even though I've never been one. The other challenge is to never want to sound as if I'm just feeding you a line. You've heard your share of lines.

All through my life I have gravitated to female friendships. I walk down the street and women who are complete strangers smile at me. Well, maybe it's not so surprising. I guess just about everyone loves a grandpa, and that's probably what they see—an old, bald, overweight, hard-of-hearing grandpa. Even though they don't know it, I hope what they can see, as I smile back at them, is God's unconditional love flowing through my eyes.

My business is advertising, and I sometimes find myself in the reception rooms of television and radio stations waiting for a salesperson. The receptionist and I begin to talk, and if there's no one else around, often it isn't long before she's in tears, telling me about her divorce, her awful husband, or her rebellious kids. When people come in, she stops telling her story and returns to her work, but as soon as they leave, she continues. I never have a clue about what I say to start this flow, except that I expressed an interest in her as a person and listened to her.

Barb and I sometimes do women's conferences where I'm the only man. Once we did one for Bible teacher Kay Arthur. Five hundred women were at her ranch for a retreat. All those women. I felt as if I'd died and gone to heaven. Since I'm old and harmless, the women felt free to open up and discuss problems they were having with their husbands, including delicate aspects of the relationship. I listened and tried to interpret what their men might be thinking. After the seminar, a number of women asked Barb if they could take me home since I was already trained!

Just because I have lots of female friends doesn't mean I don't have male friends. I've had hundreds. It's just that my life has always seemed to have lots of women in it, and I don't mean in a sexual way. I know you've had male "friends" who had other things in mind in addition to being friends, but I hope that through the pages of this book, you'll feel secure with me as we laugh and cry about some sensitive issues.

I realize you sometimes think men are thickheaded, insensitive, one-dimensional, self-centered, and obsessed with sex. Well, you're right—basically, at least. That seems to be the way most of them appear. There's good news, though. Most men *can* be assembled into people who are caring, nurturing, self-sacrificing, and sensitive. They just need someone to teach them how to incorporate these traits into their lives.

Once in a while the teacher can be the wife, but in my opinion that rarely happens. In fact, the Bible says a wife shouldn't even TRY to teach her husband. Most of the time you need a third party to help you understand a man and hear what he is saying. This third party should usually be someone a little older who has courage enough to be real and let down his guard and admit he, too, has made mistakes. Gary Smalley was my third party. Barb and I met him years ago when we began working with Pro Athletes Outreach. When I'd tell Gary about some of Barb's complaints, he was not afraid to be vulnerable and tell stories about himself to illustrate his points. He'd slap his leg and say, "That's just what Norma used to say about me."

Usually, a wife cannot be her husband's "third party." We men tend to get defensive when someone tries to tell us what to do or gives us what we think is criticism. From a woman's standpoint, she doesn't mean to criticize. She is simply offering a helpful little hint that would help him better meet her needs. She knows he would want to have that piece of information since he loves her. But he reacts like he's been hit with a two by four.

Perhaps through the pages of this book I can help you understand that a man's actions are just the nature of the "beast" and not some personal vendetta or an uncaring attitude toward you. More than anything, I want to give you hope that when you and God get your team together, a man can be changed. He can become all that you hoped he'd be and, more important, everything that God *wants* him to be.

A word of caution. In a book like this I must write in a very general way. Not all men are exactly alike. If the man in your life is not like the men I describe, and you have no trouble understanding him, congratulations! Give this book to someone who needs it. Obviously, your man is one of the exceptions in our world, and you are blessed. (There *are* sensitive men. There's one guy in Sioux Falls and another in Pensacola, but those are the only two I know anything about.)

You won't always agree with my thoughts; even after you read this book, there may be some things you *still* don't understand about how a man thinks. My hope is that through my being vulnerable, real, and honest about my life, you will be able to gain valuable insights on how a man is designed.

Men need some tinkering, adjusting, arranging, completing, conforming, sorting, straightening, fine-tuning, connecting, balancing, focusing, overhauling, sharpening, grinding, building, patching up, restoring, framing, solidifying, troubleshooting, renewing, polishing, calibrating, mending, and reshaping; because with *men, some assembly is required.*

I'm honored you would take the time to read this book. I hope you'll have some fun as we explore the mysterious caverns of a man's mind. Better wear your boots, though. It might get a little muddy.

With God's love,

Chuck Snyder

A Word from Barb

Chuck is a tease! Chuck has a wonderful sense of humor! Chuck exaggerates!

When I was young, I thought about the type of man I would like to marry, and he was just like Chuck is today—without the exaggerations. I wanted someone with whom I could be friends. I wanted us to have lots of fun together. I wanted someone who would listen and who could talk intelligently. I wanted someone sensitive.

I got someone sensitive—very sensitive. After we were married for a time, he would tease, and I would tease him back. Then a veil would drop over his face, and all of sudden, it was not teasing anymore, it was serious. Now, mind you, he continued to tease me, but I could no longer tease him. I believe this happened because both of us did things to hurt each other, without even meaning to. Somehow Chuck took the teasing personally and thought I was out to "get him." He would think the worst about himself and assume I was thinking the same way. When we talked about it, he would tell me what I was thinking, but he would use "his" vocabulary. I used to tell him I was on his side.

At the point in our lives when we realized what he was doing, Chuck put two and two together by remembering the scripture that says, "Love is not irritable or touchy. . . . If you love someone you will be loyal to him no matter what the cost. You will always believe in him, always expect the best of him, and always stand your ground in defending him" (1 Cor. 13:5-7).

One of the things I admire most about this man I married is his obedience to the Lord when he discovers he has been disobedient. So Chuck took the scripture to heart and began to believe that I love him and teasing is just teasing and not an attempt to hurt him. As the years have passed—40 this year—we have matured and come to believe the best about each other.

So Chuck and I tease back and forth all the time. What he does in this book when he tells stories about me is the norm in our house. I know he would never do anything to hurt me nor would I ever hurt him. I know he loves me, and so I don't want you to worry about me if you think his jokes are not as funny as he thinks they are. I love his jokes and enjoy them just as much as he does.

On the other hand, there WERE times in our past when he told the stories wrong, he told them too soon, and he hadn't gotten the point of why something had happened. Some assembly WAS required in those instances, and he assembled real well.

I just want you to know that Chuck has my approval for this book, even though if I were telling the story, it might have been told differently.

Barb Snyder

1

How in the World Did I End Up with an Opposite?

Why can't a woman be more like a man? So the song from *My Fair Lady* goes. Wouldn't life be a whole lot simpler if men and women thought alike, responded in the same way, had the same interests and tastes? When you were dating, perhaps you thought you and the person who became your spouse were very much alike. I want to tell you the world's best-kept secret. No woman is supposed to know it, but I'm going to let you in on it anyway because you deserve an explanation. But first, so you'll understand what it is I'm talking about, I want to tell you my story.

I think I began to notice girls around the third grade. Before that I knew they existed but I had no idea what purpose they served, other than being the first ones to raise their hands in class and never getting in trouble.

Then Jean Trovani moved into the seat behind me, and I began bringing chocolate chip cookies from home to show I cared. Well, my romance with Jean didn't go anywhere, but it's a nice memory.

It was high school before I got up the courage to have a real girlfriend. I made a few tentative overtures, and when she reciprocated, I panicked and quickly faded into the sunset. I feel bad about that even today, but the feeling of commitment scared me.

I spent summers helping my grandfather and uncles on the farm. I did chores and field work for them. Grandmother hired young girls to help her prepare meals and do the shopping. It was a delight to come in from the fields to such visions of loveliness. They looked terrific and smelled great, and once in a while my heart leaped within me because our elbows touched at the dinner table.

I remember one time when I was about 16, the hired girl and I decided to see what it felt like to stay out all night and watch the sun rise. Believe it or not, we did nothing either of us is ashamed of. We just wanted to see the sun come up over a beautiful rock canyon near Coulee City, Washington. We slept a little, we waited a long time, and sure enough, pretty soon here came the sun. And then sure enough, pretty soon here came my uncle and aunt in their car.

There was just one little bitty problem with our staying out all night. We had forgotten to tell my uncle and aunt about it. I guess I would have told them if it had ever occurred to me there would be a problem. They had spent most of the night looking for us. I'm sure they had visions of us in a car that had gone over a bank or into a lake or maybe had been wrecked on the road. I'm so sorry, but kids do dumb stuff like that, and that was one of my dumbest!

Can you believe they didn't yell at us? They were relieved that we were safe. However, we both had to work all day. Just because we had pulled a dumb stunt didn't mean the weeds had taken a vacation, or the animals didn't need to be fed, or the fields worked. I can still remember nodding off as I drove the tractor that day. We even got some teasing during dinner that evening, but that was it.

Unconditional love after a stupid stunt like that. What a gift to young lives! How did they learn about unconditional love? Maybe because they were getting a little older but could still remember some of the dumb things they had done as kids.

Just a few years after this incident, I decided to go to Washington State College (now University) in Pullman, Washington, and become a veterinarian. The first week of my freshman year, I was reading the bulletin board in the dorm and saw an advertisement saying a country music band needed a guitar player. I auditioned, got the job, and began playing music every Friday night and Saturday night for Granges, barn dances, and socials at various campus dormitories, fraternities, sororities, and other living groups. It was good clean fun, and the students seemed to like the change of pace from the popular music of the day.

I fell in love with the girl singer in the band, but she already had a boyfriend, so that was the end of that. Once, however, she invited our band to come to her sorority and entertain the girls at a Sunday lunch. I sat across the table from a little doll who immediately captured my attention. Before the meal was over, she left with a hunk, and I hadn't even learned her name. Oh well, easy come, easy go.

I found out later that the name of the little doll who walked out on me that day was Barb, and she called her mom to say she had found the man she was going to marry—*me*, not the hunk! I felt the same way about her, but since I was so shy, I really didn't have a clue how to follow up my feelings.

The lunch at which we met was in May. After the school year I was scheduled for a YMCA-YWCA conference where I was to serve as co-chairman. Barb had planned to go home to Wenatchee after the year was over, but when she found out I was cochairman, she registered for the conference.

The first day of the conference, my shoes were all wet from tromping around the grounds and making sure everything was set up. I asked Barb if she would drive with me the short distance to my home in Tacoma for some dry shoes. We didn't have stoves in those days, I guess, or at least it didn't enter my mind to dry them out over a stove. When I got to my home, I left Barb in the car, and I ran in to get the shoes. I didn't see the necessity of introducing my folks to a girl I had met only twice. Since I hadn't dated much when I was living at home, having a girl in the car was a shock to my mom's system. She reported later how many aspirin tablets she had to take to get to sleep that night.

We drove back to the conference, and the next day began trying to solve the problems of the world. We had committees on war and peace, atomic weapons testing, and lots of social concerns. Since I was cochairman, I could monitor any of the committees I chose, and by the sheerest coincidence, I chose the committees on which Barb was serving. To make a short story shorter, by Tuesday of that week we were engaged. By Friday we had our wedding planned; however, we didn't tell anyone because stories like ours happened only in the movies.

When we returned to school the next fall, instead of showing off her engagement ring, Barb put it in her house mother's trunk. She was just waiting for the right time to tell everyone. I was just waiting for time, period. In the olden days a couple had to wait until both of them had an evening free to announce the engagement to both their living groups at the same time. I had so many activities going I couldn't find an evening free. But somehow we managed to find lots of time to be together.

My whole life was wrapped up in being with Barb because we had so much in common. She loved country music, or at least it appeared that way, because she took her handiwork wherever I was playing with the band and sat there with a smile on her face. I went well out of my way to walk her to her next class. I pretended to like vegetables. I also thought only Chinese people drank tea, but I put 15 spoons of sugar in it and managed to get it down. I went with her to the Apple Blossom Parade in her hometown. I loved to meet her in the library to study. I didn't want to leave her for a minute, and the saddest part of my day happened when I had to leave her at the back door of her sorority house. We both looked forward to the time when we'd not have to say good-bye, but when we could go, instead, to our own apartment.

The point of all my dating stories is to explain that as is the case with most couples, I was looking for someone exactly like me. And I found her! Her name was Barb. We had so much in common. We were completely compatible.

Then we got married . . . and all of a sudden, we found out we were **OPPOSITES**. In fact, we discovered we were the Most Opposite Couple in the World.

Barb suddenly decided she didn't like country music. I didn't bother to pretend that I liked vegetables. I just passed the plate by and drank coffee. I also had better things to do than watch apple blossom displays that looked the same every year. Over the years we began keeping track of all the differences we found, and we now have two single-spaced 8 1/2-by-11-inch sheets of paper. We hand them to people who want to challenge us for the "Most Opposite" title. What happened?

The Mystery

Barb experienced one of the mysteries many of you might have experienced. That is, you seem to have married two different men. The man you dated was caring and loving. He opened doors for you and stood up when you returned to the table at a restaurant. He looked deeply into your eyes and said things like, "Tell me more about that," "Isn't that interesting," and "What else did your mother say?" He was excited about going shopping with you, and he waited patiently while you tried on shoes or examined blouses. He knew when you needed a hug and encouragement, and he didn't try to "fix" your feelings. He just listened and reflected your feelings back to you in his own words. He was interested in what you were interested in.

Maybe your family had always gone to the state fair during your growing-up years, and you loved the cross-stitch exhibit and the agricultural barn where they put fresh fruit in patterns. When you told your boyfriend about it, he said, "Be still my heart," because that sounded like so much fun. He made a date with you for next September so you could enjoy the fair together. He even marked it down in his Day-Timer and circled it in red so he couldn't possibly forget. Yes, your boyfriend went to the symphony with you, enjoyed sitting on a blanket by the lake, and loved finding out about your day, your goals, and your current problems.

He also made encouraging sounds as you were talking: "Uh-huh . . . Oh . . . Umm." He looked directly into your eyes, and you saw into his soul. He washed your car on Saturday and helped your dad spade the garden. He charmed your mother so she could hardly wait for the wedding, knowing full well that her future son-in-law was one of a kind. She was always giving him the extra piece of pie or letting him have the sports page first on Sunday.

Your dad, however, was probably not quite as convinced. Isn't it funny that a young man who is not worthy of a daughter's hand can later participate in creating the Most Perfect Grandchildren in the World? Your dad liked the "kid" but hoped he would cut his hair, shave off the beard, dump the earring, take the mattress out of his VW van, or put a more comfortable seat for you on his Harley. "And don't you *dare* visit his apartment alone!" Dad warned.

Even if a dating couple should happen to discover a difference of opinion on something, they don't say, "That's dumb!" They say, "That's an interesting viewpoint. I don't think I've ever seen it quite that way. Tell me more about how you feel."

The wedding day comes, and you, the bride, look forward to a lifetime of blissful communication and companionship. You don't suspect that anything could happen to your husband while you change your dress after the ceremony. But it isn't long until you know something has definitely happened. What?

For the first time I'll reveal the deep, dark secret. Your new husband has had brain surgery. It occurs right after the reception, before you leave on your honeymoon. The church usually has a clinic set up in the Christian education room or nursery. While you change clothes, your husband is whisked into the room. A doctor carefully opens up his brain cavity and begins his exacting work. First of all, he replaces the "visiting" lobe with the "Monday Night Football" lobe. Then he replaces the "caring" lobe with a "career" lobe. He replaces the "feeling" lobe with a "doing" lobe. Finally, he replaces the "shopping" lobe with a "sports" lobe, and then he sews him back up.

When you see your new husband again, he's a completely different man. His new brain tells him he has accomplished one of his lifetime goals. He has married you. With that accomplished, he is now on to bigger and better things, like his work or sports or hobbies. No longer does he ask how you feel. When you look into his eyes, not only can you no longer see his soul, but there isn't even anyone home. His eyes now look like glazed-over grapefruit halves. He never quite gets to fixing the seat for you on his Harley. When you remind him of the state fair, he has no interest because he saw it once, so why would he want to see it again? The fruit patterns in the agricultural barn and all the animals look the same as they did the first time he was there. And he doesn't even know what a cross-stitch is, let alone want to see an exhibit.

He now gives you solutions in exchange for your feelings and tries to "fix" you. He burps and scratches and does other things that offend you. McDonald's is the closest you come to a fancy restaurant—that is, when you can even get him to take you out. His eyes go blank when you talk about your mother. He hates the symphony, and you find that *his* "classical" entertainers are Merle Haggard, Ronnie Milsap, and Ricky Skaggs—and that he wants them entertaining at 500 decibels in the car or family room through his six-foot speakers. You have to wash your own car. He doesn't have time to visit. He no longer looks into your eyes, and he now disagrees with you on everything. He thinks you're wrong, and suddenly you discover hundreds of differences between the two of you. Somehow they escaped you completely while you were dating.

Your husband doesn't even go shopping with you anymore, or if he does, he is what Barb calls me, a "presence" or "pressure." But let me say, I think I'm paying Barb a high honor even to *go* shopping. My whole life comes screeching to a dead stop when I shop with her. No longer can I change the world. I have to stand around while Barb compares blouses or shoe colors. She has a pair of shoes in every style and color ever made, but none of them is comfortable, and she's always looking for Nirvana Shoes that we never quite find.

A few caring stores have husband comfort stations consisting of one overstuffed chair somewhere, but I really believe that most want to inflict additional pain on the man for his original sin of not refusing the apple in the Garden of Eden, so they make him stand. And even if he's fortunate enough to beat to the one chair the other 15 men waiting for their wives, he is stuck with reading magazines like *Hairdos of the World*, *Blouse of the Month Journal*, or the *Women's Prairie Companion*, with articles titled "Skirt Styles I Have Loved."

There's Hope

I'm so sorry about your husband's brain surgery. But part of the purpose of this book is to help you see that you can't do much about the problem. That's no excuse to stop reading this book, however. There *is* hope that a third party will come into your husband's life and teach him how to be the caring, loving, compassionate person you thought you were marrying. Unfortunately, most men have no one to teach them how to meet a woman's needs. In most cases, fathers and grandfathers have not been taught by their own fathers and grandfathers what it means to be a loving husband. Even the church fathers haven't been much help, although the Bible is clear on how a husband is to treat his wife.

There is a ray of sunshine, so keep turning the pages, and by the time I finish this letter to you, you'll have an idea of the part you can play in this building project. I'll explain why your husband thinks about sex all the time. Why he doesn't value relationships as much as you do. Why he doesn't quite get to the household repairs as quickly as you want him to. Why he doesn't notice when you get your hair done. Why his work can be as destructive as the "other" woman. Why your husband is so focused. Why he doesn't hear you when you talk to him. Why most of the men in your life are fanatics about watching sports on TV. What a man's greatest fears are. Why he takes your helpful hints as criticism. Why he won't go to the doctor. And how to release your husband so he will come toward you and not run away.

By the time you finish this book you'll have lots of hope, but right now, your marriage has taken place, and you realize to your horror that you and your husband are *different*. So what's a woman to do?

2

God Said We Were "One Flesh" and I'm the One . . . Right?

The only Scriptures I had during my growing-up years were the Dead Sea Scrolls. And in Genesis 2:18, in one of the Dead Sea Scrolls, God referred to the woman as the man's "helpmeet." No one seemed to know exactly what that meant. It sounded as if the woman was to be the man's helper, following him around the world, picking up his underwear and socks, having his dinner ready on time, and jumping into bed with him any time he was in the mood.

Barb has a gift for teaching and through her I learned that the original Hebrew word for "helpmeet " was *completer*. That put a whole different spin on my perception of Barb's role in my life. If she was going to *complete* me, that implied that she had to be different than I am. Amazing! I guess I took the Bible literally when it said the man and the wife were "one flesh" in marriage. But I thought I was the "one," since I am mostly right, at least from my enlightened viewpoint. Since I was "right" and I was one flesh with Barb, I thought that would greatly simplify things for her. All she had to do was look at things my way, and we'd have the most perfect marriage ever.

Therefore, when we got married and became one flesh, I was sure my vacation plans would be *our* vacation plans. My furniture preferences would be *our* furniture preferences. My favorite entertainment would be *our* favorite entertainment. However, I discovered I had married someone almost completely my opposite in every way. I was totally bewildered. No one had warned me that when two people are dating, they become blind to reality.

Not all couples are totally different. Some marriage partners are more the same than the opposite of each other. If that's your situation, you're not weird, just rare. But it doesn't mean you don't have conflicts. It means you and your husband have different *kinds* of conflicts from the couples who are so opposite.

At first, I really thought God had made a big mistake creating Barb so different. I had no doubt she was meant to be my lifetime partner, but I found we had only one thing in common: We were married on the same day! That was it. Oh, and Barb reminds me we also have the same children and grandchildren. Those are the only similarities. How did I miss the fact that we were so different? You already know the answer from our discussion in the chapter on dating. We were sharing only similarities, not differences, during our courtship.

Since I always thought I was right about most everything, one of the biggest shocks to me was the realization that Barb thought I was *wrong* most of the time. But since I got the impression from my parents and the churches in which I grew up that anger and conflict were sins, I just stuffed my feelings and went along with Barb's program. She was not aware that she ever did anything wrong in my eyes. As I think back on those days, I didn't look at her as wrong, either. Subconsciously, that would have set up an impossible situation. If I had thought she was wrong, that would have meant we might have conflict, which would have meant I might be angry, which would have meant I would sin, and I was supposed to try not to sin. So I focused on work and tried not to notice when she did something "wrong." I didn't know yet that she wasn't right or wrong, but that she was *different* from me. I was just avoiding conflict so I didn't sin.

I came from a very quiet family. No one ever raised a voice, and we surely didn't express a difference of opinion. Thinking back, I can remember times when my dad would get quiet or tense up a bit, but I never took that as anger. A person shouted and threw things if he was angry. As I think about our family life, I can see that my mom was quite dominant, so I'm sure there *were* times when Dad went into his garage and kicked the Model A Ford. But I never saw it.

Barb, on the other hand, had a family whose members showed their feelings more openly. They could stand toe to toe, have a shouting match filled with anger, and then be friends again quickly. So when Barb and I got together and had a disagreement, I thought we had failed horribly and I felt bad. But she thought we had succeeded wonderfully, and she felt great!

I mentioned that Barb and I have two single-spaced pages that spell out how we are different. We list our differences in our book called *Incompatibility: Grounds for a Great Marriage*, [1] and we keep adding to the list. For instance, since we've been teaching together, I've noticed that Barb takes notes in *pencil,* if you can believe that. I think God would have us take notes in ink, and my preference is a blue Flair pen with a broad point that lets me make a statement to the world and stand behind it, never to change or give in. Barb's pencil says that she might change her mind or give in to someone else's opinion and so she might need to erase something.

She also likes the window in our bedroom open. I like it closed because it lets in bugs and pollen, which makes me sneeze. We have a water fountain outside our bedroom window that makes noise. Barb needs to have it shut off at night so she can't hear it. I suggested we just shut the window so she can't hear the fountain, and then we wouldn't have an extra thing to remember. She decided she likes the window open, and now I do a lot of sneezing.

Barb wants all the clocks set on "real time." I want them all set seven minutes fast so I won't be late for things. Five minutes wouldn't work for me because it's too easy to compute. If my watch is seven minutes fast, it's more complicated to figure out what time it really is, so I just leave for a meeting when my watch says time to go.

Barb is into "guidelines," not deadlines. She sees no reason to be somewhere on time since meetings always start late anyway. She swears she's always on time, but she isn't. I try to ease her kitchen clock ahead to a more comfortable time, but she has just installed a new microwave and a new oven, and both have digital clocks. At a glance she can compare the three clocks and see if I've been messing with one of them.

I'm what is known as a "progressive sleeper." That means I like to have three alarm clocks set to wake me up in the morning. I put one by the bed, and when it goes off, I know I still have a half hour to sleep, so I can peacefully doze off again. I put the second one where I have to stretch for it a bit, and when it goes off, I know I have 15 more minutes of blissful sleep. I put the third one on the dresser. When it goes off, I have to actually get up to shut it off, and as long as I'm up, I might as well go to work. The problem is, Barb bolts straight up at alarm number one and is awake for the rest of the day. She's not crazy about the three-alarm system, so I have gone to just one.

However, this has created a major problem for me because I'm getting hard of hearing and need the alarm clock close to the bed. In contrast, Barb has the world's best hearing and can hear a single leaf "clicking" off its branch somewhere in our four acres of woods. I don't mind the ticking of a clock. It's kind of peaceful. So we have this routine. I set the alarm clock on the bedside table on my side of the bed and begin to read my book.

"I can still hear it," she reports. So I put it on the floor beside the bed. "I can still hear it," she says. So I put a pillow over it. "I can still hear it," she says again. So I move it out to the garage. "I can still hear it," she insists. So I move it out to the woods, and finally, she can't hear it anymore and we can go to sleep. The obvious problem is that now I have to stay awake all night worrying about whether I'll get up on time because I won't be able to hear the alarm clock in the woods.

I also stayed awake nights worrying about whether I snore. At least I did before I moved into another bedroom—something about Barb never getting any sleep. So in our old age, at least both of us are getting our sleep now and I can hear the alarm, but I doubt we'll have any more babies.

We traditionally spend New Year's Eve with two of Barb's brothers and their wives at a cabin on the water. Our home is 7,000 square feet. The cabin is about 400 square feet. It takes a little getting used to. We have a good time, just the six of us. However, several years ago, Barb's brother Dick invited the entire town of Edmonds to stay overnight and celebrate. Barb and I usually sleep in a loft area, but that year there were men, women, and children all over the place, invading my space. And to make things worse, a couple hundred people were going to share the loft with us at night, including another brother, Phil, and his wife, Max. I went up on the roof where no one could see me put on my pajamas (I couldn't get into the bathroom because of the hundreds of people already there) and sneaked into bed as all the rest of the people were finally settling down.

Now came the snoring problem. Barb suggested that if I so much as snorted even once, she was getting a divorce. Well, maybe she didn't say that, but that was how seriously I took the admonition not to snore. I lay there staring at the ceiling, contemplating my fate. To sleep and lose a wife, or to stay awake and not snore—those seemed to be my only options.

Then a rumbling began to shake the foundation of the cabin, and it kept getting louder and louder. It was Phil and

Max. *They* were snoring, Barb was breathing hard in her sleep, too, and I was in big trouble. I did doze off once, but Barb awoke, punched me, and then went back to sleep. That was probably the worst night of my life. Fortunately, last year the crowd was reduced to the six of us again, but I find myself not being a success in life because of the constant fear that my septuagint will flap over my occidental—or whatever happens that makes me snore.

Barb wants me to get my throat cut. Well, that's not quite how she describes it. I guess there's a laser procedure now where they make some incisions in the septuagint or something. The problem is, you can't talk the rest of your life, and since I make my living doing radio and TV commercials, I just can't see risking a fly-by-night procedure that would put us on food stamps.

Another of our differences is that Barb balances her checkbook to the penny and I have what I call my "E factor." When I get my statement from the bank, I check to see if we agree on how much I have in the account. If the bank says I have a little more than I thought, I just put E in my bank book and add the difference. If the checkbook says I have a little less than I thought, I just put E in my bank book and subtract the difference. I come out to the *penny* every time. I know exactly how much I have in the account. I figure if I'm within $20 of agreeing, who wants to spend his sunset years looking for why that happened? It was someone's mistake, either mine or the bank's, so I just use the E (error) factor and get on with my life.

Barb and I even found we have different spiritual gifts and study the Bible differently. Barb has a teacher's gift and spends *hours* sitting in her chair checking out the word tenses and matching verse with verse. And she doesn't like counseling. I have the gift of exhortation and spend *minutes* in the Bible between client meetings, in bathrooms, and at lunch. And I *love* counseling.

One of the most fun things I do (that doesn't involve Barb) is going to lunch with a couple experiencing marriage problems, people who are complete strangers to me and, even better, non-

Christians. Non-Christians are so much fun. They don't know what they don't believe, and they've never heard of such concepts as serving, giving up rights, honoring the other person, and looking out for number *two*. They've also never experienced unconditional love from a far-right, fundamentalist, weirdo, born-again Christian.

Our differences are evident even when we are preparing for one of our marriage seminars. Since Barb is a teacher, she wants to have an outline when we speak. Since I'm an exhorter, I'm comfortable just reading the Scriptures involved and telling the people how to apply them to their lives.

Once, after we did a Saturday seminar at a church, the pastor wanted us to stay and speak to a Sunday school class the next morning. I'm easy, so I thought it would be a great opportunity to talk with more people about what we've learned. Barb went along with the idea, even though it wasn't her preference. In private, she asked what we were going to do. I took out the little idea sheet I always have in my pocket, listed four scripture passages on suffering, and gave them to her as I said, "Christians don't know how to handle trials in a God-honoring way, so let's talk about suffering."

"What's our plan?" she said.

"Our plan is to read these verses and apply them to their lives."

"What's our outline?"

"Our outline is to read these verses and apply them to their lives."

"What's our goal?"

"Our goal is to read these verses and apply them to their lives."

Our discussion ended when she said, "You handle it," meaning she would have nothing to say and I could wing it. "Wing it" to her means not having a plan. "Wing it" to me is not being tied to a specific outline and using the Bible rather than notes to apply the principles to the listeners' lives.

The next morning, I was prepared to wing it. Barb was

prepared not to say anything except maybe to amplify something I said. When we got in front of the group, I said, "Good morning," and Barb broke in and for 45 minutes taught all the things the Holy Spirit had been teaching her over the past 20 years. I asked her to take a breath once in a while so I could add something. Both of our gifts were in action, and we fit together great because we're different.

We were studying for a presentation once and paused to compare our notes. I was trying to find ways to make the audience laugh. Barb wanted to present some insights. Now, I think there's no better way to learn something than to laugh—especially when the teachers laugh at themselves. Barb wants to give a lot of information. Neither of us is right or wrong; we're just different.

Our approach to hotels is another area where our differences show up. When we started doing some traveling and would get to a hotel, the person at the front desk would give us the key for room 203. I'm into the sovereignty of God big-time, so I would assume that God, before the foundation of the earth, had determined that Barb and I should be in room 203.

Barb didn't seem to share that concept, however, especially when we got to room 203. The room didn't smell good. It was too close to the elevator. The bed was the wrong size. Happy hour in the bar under our room made too much noise. We couldn't see the ocean, and so on. While I thought God wanted us to be in room 203, Barb wanted to *change rooms,* if you can imagine such a thing. I was so embarrassed. She actually wanted to go down to the front desk, interrupt the important work the person was doing, and ask for keys to 15 different rooms so she could choose the one she wanted. I tried to stay out of sight so no one knew she belonged to me. Later, when she had decided on a room, I would sneak up the fire escape and we'd settle in.

Then I found out she has the *gift* of hotels. She can interrupt the flow of commerce without a twinge of guilt, and we do end up with a better room. Now when we check in, I give her the charge card and head for the nearest soft chair, where I can read the book I always carry with me for this sort of situation. She does all the negotiating for the correct room, and I'm the one who gets a better view of the ocean. Works great!

Barb also has the gift of navigation. I seldom know where I am except when I drive to work. Even though I knew instinctively that she's a better navigator than I am, I would still get irritated when Barb would say, "Why didn't you turn back there? You missed the exit. Why are you going this way?" I had no good answers for her questions, so I would feel put down. Barb didn't intend to make me feel put down. She just knew the best way to get there and thought I should, too.

Finally, I realized I wasn't the best navigator in the family; Barb was. And I turned all that over to her. I made a rule: Barb was to be in charge of navigation any time we were in the car together. She was to do this by saying, "Turn right," or "Turn left." I told her I would be writing commercials or building furniture in my mind while I was driving, so it was up to her to make sure we got where we were going. This is not an exaggeration. One time she coughed, and I turned right. The street to the left was blocked, so I knew she couldn't have meant for me to turn that way.

She broke the rules not long ago. We were traveling down this road toward the water. I saw a sign that said "Dead End," and I reported this to Barb. She agreed she had also seen a sign that said "Dead End." She had not said, "Turn right," or "Turn left," however, so I went straight ahead—into the dead end. I figured she knew something I didn't. When I got to the end of the road, I stopped and reported once again to Barb, "This is a dead end." She agreed it was a dead end and added, ""What in the world are we doing here!" She hadn't told me to turn right or left, so what did she expect? The only option was to keep going straight. Barb thought I should have known by then where the ferry dock was. I didn't. I just turn right or left when she tells me.

Both Barb and I thought we had the gift of airports. So we used to have a conflict every time we arrived at an out-of-town airport. I think we should get the rental car first because the luggage takes time to be unloaded. She thinks we should wait for the luggage so it won't be stolen. And when we are flying out, I think we should go right to the gate. Barb sometimes wants to stop for coffee and see how close we can come to the departure time by going through the security gate just as the plane starts to taxi, or at least that's how it seems to me.

One time we went through the airport mess and out to the gate without a single conflict. It was wonderful. I commented on this amazing fact, and Barb said, "That's because I did everything *your* way." I was glad she finally recognized my gift of airports.

It's Hard Work

I think you get the point that marriage takes a lot of work, especially if you are different from your marriage partner.

Although we've been deeply influenced by and are eternally grateful to people like Dr. Jim Dobson, Gary Smalley, Larry Burkett, Kay Arthur, Larry Wright, and Dr. Norm Wright, most of the ideas we pass along about marriage have not been learned from books. Actually, I've learned most of my marriage lessons through my MISTAKES! Because I am a typical man who hates to fail, you'd think I would be reluctant to share the things I did wrong. However, I have found that only through sharing my mistakes can I give other people insights into how to have a better marriage. Since Barb and I have filtered the principles through our lives, we know they work, and we can now turn around and share with others the same comfort God gave us during our hard times.

If we had tried to get out of all our problems, we would have little of value to say to other couples. It's easy to run away when the going gets rough in a marriage, as so many people are doing these days. It's hard to stick around and work through the problems.

Having said that, let me quickly acknowledge that solving marriage problems is not simple. Marriage problems are infinitely complex. They spring from differences in parenting, schooling, personalities, learning styles, cultures, and men-women differences, to name just a few. I've counseled hundreds of couples, and the problems are never clear-cut nor is one person mostly to blame. I can't think of any greater agony on this earth than marriage conflict. And part of the struggle is the mental question we have as to how something that started out so sweet and wonderful could end up in such bitterness and hate.

Some of you reading this book have experienced the hell of divorce, abandonment, emotional or physical abuse. Even though I can't feel your pain, I want you to know I wish things had turned out different for you. Please do not feel I'm putting you down in what I'm saying here. I'm just suggesting that when *both* people in a marriage can put their differences aside and begin to learn how to meet the other person's needs, and begin a good-faith effort to change, there are hope and healing for the relationship. Sometimes professional counseling plays a part in the healing process, but often good results can be had by counseling with another couple who have had similar struggles and have overcome them.

So far I have never found such a thing as a "perfect" marriage. There will always be some areas of growth that pinch a little bit. Part of the solution is finding out what the Bible has to say about marriage, reading books, listening to tapes, and attending marriage seminars. All these help us begin to hone the necessary skills to do our part in making the relationship everything God wants it to be. Once again let me say that I realize there are no simple answers to marriage conflict. But I know from my own experience that God can make diamonds out of ashes when we use His principles as the basis for our efforts.

Coming together in marriage is like two streams flowing side by side and then blending. When the streams come together, there is a great deal of foam and splashing. However, as they become one, they are stronger and deeper than either one of them was individually.

I find that in marriages where I'm asked to help, the blending of those two streams of differences causes the most frequent problem. To help the couple understand their differences, I give the Taylor-Johnson Temperament Analysis®[1]. It's a wonderful test that charts nine different personality opposites. It gives me clear insight into who has the "blue Mondays." It shows me who is the party animal and who doesn't even want to go to the mailbox. It explains why the couple can't communicate and why they tend to give each other solutions rather than empathy. It tells me who is reading negative feelings into situations and always comes up with the wrong answer. It shows which one can make wise decisions based on facts rather than feelings. It shows who is running over whom, who is angry, and who wants the magazines on the coffee table equidistant from the edges and sorted by date.

When Barb and I took this test, it was the first time we understood how very different we are. If you've never taken it or you took it before marriage, I suggest you call around to the Christian counselors in your area and find one to give you this test. It was a life-changer for us, and I recommend it highly.

The biggest struggle of marriage partners is allowing the other person to be who God designed him or her to be. The marriage relationship is so intimate that we know each other's strong points, weak points, and kind of deodorant the other uses. Because of unrealistic expectations prior to marriage, it isn't long before the husband and the wife begin emphasizing what the partner is doing "wrong" rather than catching the partner doing things "right." And once the differences become the focal point of a marriage, most of the relationship is bound up with "She always . . ." or "He never . . ."

I grieve when couples come to me after having been in counseling for years and have little or no progress to show for their time. In my experience, they usually have so little to celebrate because the counselor or pastor has been dealing with *symptoms* rather than the *root problem*, which is that the couple is not being obedient to the biblical principles of marriage. In general, solving most marriage problems takes a lot of hard work especially if there are complicating factors like abusive childhood, addictions, divorced parents, and so on. Some of those things require counseling before you can even get to the subject of marriage.

God has given some specific instructions in the Bible on how to pull off a harmonious, satisfying marriage, and a majority of people will be able to do it if they do things God's way. The hard part of marriage is giving up the selfish nature: thinking of the other person first; serving the mate; meeting his or her needs; learning how to be friends, lovers, and partners. It's all there in the Book if people will be open to doing what God says.

Let me add a quick word to those of you who have been divorced. Many of you have been rejected after doing everything you could to keep the marriage together, and some of you had to walk away because of physical abuse or habitual adultery. I wish I could give you a big, old, grandfatherly hug, but I can't. So the next best thing is to remind you that God has promised to be a father to the fatherless and a husband to the husbandless, and He is committed to being your comfort through the pains of this life. One of the ways you can help make diamonds out of ashes is to be quick to share your story with other people going through the same thing. You can be God's instrument of hope to help them survive the same trauma in their lives.

The Stuff Dreams Are Made Of

The marriage process involves continual growth and learning. It's typical to assume that once your partner shapes up, learns more about what's "right," and becomes a little more like you, you can dust off your hands and announce that your marriage is everything it should be and you can now get on to other things. Well, I have news. You will *never* change a man into your own image (nor will he change you into his). He will *never* see things exactly as you do. He will *always* do things that irritate you. The sooner you relax and accept God's plan, which involves differences between you and your husband, the sooner you can begin building your marriage into the stuff dreams are made of.

The helpmeet (completion) idea in Genesis 2:18 also speaks to me of equality. Barb completes me and brings gifts and character strengths to our relationship that I don't have. I complete her and bring gifts and character strengths to our relationship that she doesn't have. We both submit ourselves to God, and Barb and I become a unit: one flesh—not two, or slightly two, or a little bit two. We are *one* flesh; inseparable, indivisible; a single entity.

I picture the marriage relationship as a triangle. The husband serves the wife, and the wife serves the husband. They both serve God equally. But if they draw further apart from each other, they also draw further apart from God.

My goal is for you to relax to the point where you accept the differences in your marriage to such an extent that you can finally say, "Yep, he does that all the time," and "Yep, that's just the way he is." It takes a mighty dose of God's grace, but it *can* be done.

One of the areas of marital misunderstanding comes in the physical part of the relationship. Sex is a delight God has planned for married couples. But all too often, Neither partner has any idea how the other partner approaches this "icing" on the cake of marriage. So let's look at how men and women differ.

3

Sex Was God's Idea . . . Hard to Believe, Isn't it?

Barb and I were doing a marriage seminar recently. We didn't have much time left, and Barb wanted to make one more point before I began a discussion of the physical part of the relationship. So Barb said, "In a minute, Chuck will tell you everything he knows about sex." The audience, of course, broke up. After the meeting came back to order, I corrected Barb. "It will take me at least *two* minutes to tell them everything I know about sex," I said.

Did you know that the sexual relationship a man has with his wife is the most fun thing he does, and it also satisfies his greatest need? *Greatest* need. He's not some kind of animal. God gave man this intense desire and interest to make sure the human race survives. God also had another idea, and that was

25

to give a married couple the highest ecstasy this life can offer.

Yes, sex was God's idea. He thought long and hard about whether to give Adam or Eve the primary responsibility for this part of marriage. God finally chose Adam because He knew that if He trusted Eve with this important work, she would be too busy or too tired to give it much thought! If Eve had been in charge of sex, the end of the human race would have come quickly, because Eve had so many other things to think about.

On the other hand, Adam, and every man who's followed him, has been focused and one-dimensional and has expressed his eagerness to take care of this critical part of God's plan for human beings. God knew men could be trusted to do a good job. Therefore, when your husband wants to go to bed a little early once in a while, please know that it is *not* for himself. It's for the *destiny* of *mankind*, the *preservation* of the *race!* What a noble and soul-stirring burden for a man to carry! Your husband is no doubt interested in being in strict obedience to God as he carries out His mandate to preserve the human race from going down the drain because the woman is so busy. Are you convinced yet? I didn't think so. Seriously, there is more to it than that.

Sex is one of those areas of life where the man and the woman are not on the same page; often they aren't even reading the same book. For sure the motors of men start slowing down as they get into their later years (while the motors of some women start to accelerate), but even then the sexual relationship with his wife is *the* most delicious aspect of a man's life. Some people ask me if there is sex after 60. What a ridiculous question! Of course there is! My favorite time for sex is during the Christmas season, and summer is almost over, so I'm excited.

My friend, Gary Smalley, says that a man thinks about sex every 50 seconds. That's ridiculous. I don't know where he got that number. I personally have gone a minute and a half, so I know that's just not true. Just because a man thinks about sex all the time does not mean he's a beast or perverted. He's simply responding to that power charge God placed in his mind and body at creation to make sure the race continues.

Now, I'm not saying women aren't interested in sex. You just approach it differently. A glance at the covers of popular magazines tells the story. Men's magazines talk about sex as an event. Women's magazines talk about it as a relationship.

Not long ago, I was reminded of how men and women differ on sex by reading a letter a woman wrote to the editor of a local newspaper. She was ridiculing another woman writer who had been offended to see bare-breasted lesbians during a gay pride parade because of the effect it would have on male parade viewers. The writer of the letter ended her tirade by saying that *she* saw the breasts and was not suddenly filled with lustful thoughts, so how could the other woman think men would be.

I would agree with her—breasts are fairly common in a woman's world. But they're objects of great interest to men, and in our American culture, breasts have a significant sexual meaning. That's why *Playboy*, *Hustler*, and other magazines collectively make billions of dollars as they allow men to see things they're not exposed to in day-to-day life.

Even though Christian men have the same wiring as non-Christian men, we do have a different set of instructions. We don't subscribe to *Playboy* or *Hustler*. We don't sneak looks at them down at the barber shop, either. A truly committed Christian man doesn't have Showtime or HBO in his home because, first of all, he doesn't want his kids to see that sort of thing. And, second, he usually isn't able to handle all that nudity without sinning in his mind. We have to *run* from temptation. And there are many temptations in a man's life. Most hotels have porno channels. Many newsstands carry girlie magazines. Most of the movie channels feature nudity.

Even *Sports Illustrated* comes out with a swimsuit issue every year. Its purpose, of course, is to help the fashion industry sell swimming suits. (*Pause*) Now, if you believe that, please drop me a note. I have some land in Florida I'll sell you for a *great* price. The swimsuit issue is *not* about selling bathing suits; it's about selling magazines with a sexual package that's not as overt as *Playboy*. I haven't seen the figures (no pun intended), but I would bet the swimsuit issue probably results in far and away *Sports Illustrated's* greatest sales month. Why? Because men are fascinated by a woman's body. To them a woman's body is simply the most beautiful thing in the universe.

I was amused when I read a letter to the *Sports Illustrated* editor about the swimsuit issue. This well-meaning woman was mystified. "The girls in the pictures weren't even athletes," she exclaimed. She felt it would make more sense to see them in bathing suits if they had accomplished something in the swimming field. Obviously, she missed the point.

You probably thought at least *Popular Mechanics* was a safe magazine, didn't you? This might sound strange, but knowing sex sells everything else, the boat manufacturers make sure that their ads in that journal always have a man riding the waves in his boat with a knockout companion who is ready to burst out of what's laughingly called her bathing suit. But the pictures are very small. It takes a magnifying glass to really appreciate the lines—on the boat. I have to up the power on my magnifying glass constantly as I get older and my eyes get dimmer. (Barb, I'm just trying to make a point so other people can relate. I don't even *have* a magnifying glass. And even though you know I hate boats, I need to keep up with the latest innovations in case someone at the men's Bible study I teach is in the market for one, so please don't cancel my subscription.)

Even though I'm a committed Christian husband and try to be as pure-minded as I can, my eye always stops at the girl in the bathing suit who is standing by an oil filter in the *International Trucks Maintenance Manual*. I don't believe it's possible to get to the point where a man doesn't notice a beautiful woman unless he's blind, homosexual, or over 120 years old. He sees a beautiful woman as she goes down the street. He sees her and he lets it go. He doesn't go around the block, leer as she goes by, or find out her route to work and observe her every day. That would be sin.

Most people think God put Adam to sleep and instantly made woman out of one of his ribs. Well, I think that He took

His time. The superamplified Bible makes it clear through the "Aristotle" first voice of the principal tense (I have to throw some teaching terms in here so Barb will approve the book) that God stayed up late two weeks in a row working on the female form. He had some of His male angels helping. He'd mold a little clay and ask His helpers, "What do you think if I put this here?"

No response.

"How about over here?"

No response.

"What if I put a little over here?"

The male angels broke out in a little sweat.

"Perfect," said God. "Now, what would you think if We rounded off the corners a bit? In fact, My suggestion is, let's not have any sharp edges or right angles in the design at all. Smooth, soft, and round will set this product apart from the competition."

The male angels broke out in a chorus of amens.

Then God hid Eve in some bushes near where Adam was pruning the azaleas. He asked Adam to give Him some help in naming the animals and at the same time be on the lookout for a mate to complete him. Adam was completely sold out to God, so he was eager to help name the animals.

God brought out a giraffe. "Giraffe," said Adam, "but as for a mate, I don't think so." Next God had the ostrich come out and take a bow. "Ostrich," said Adam. "No on the mate thing." God brought out the kangaroo, the rhinoceros, the ant, the aardvark, and the bee. Adam kept saying the name and no. Then God brought out Eve and presented her to Adam. The King James and other translations have Adam saying "forsooth" and "verily" when he saw her. But those words just don't do justice to the emotions here. The real translation should be something like "Wow! Now You're cookin'! Whoopee! Print it! This is the one! Way to go! For sure! Perfectly rad! What a knockout!"

After Adam had recovered from his faint, God asked a couple of gorillas to hold him up, and He married the beautiful couple, who almost lived happily ever after.

A woman's body is God's exquisite handiwork. It's wholesome, and it's meant to be attractive to a man. That is God's plan. Listen to how God had Solomon describe a beautiful woman:

> How beautiful your tripping feet, O queenly maiden. Your rounded thighs are like jewels, the work of the most skilled of craftsmen. Your navel is lovely as a goblet filled with wine. Your waist is like a heap of wheat set about with lilies. Your two breasts are like two fawns, yes, lovely twins. Your neck is stately as an ivory tower, your eyes as limpid pools in Heshbon by the gate of Bath-rabbim. Your nose is shapely like the tower of Lebanon overlooking Damascus. As Mount Carmel crowns the mountains, so your hair is your crown. The king is held captive in your queenly tresses. Oh, how delightful you are; how pleasant, O love, for utter delight! You are tall and slim like a palm tree, and your breasts are like its clusters of dates. I said, I will climb up into the palm tree and take hold of its branches. Now may your breasts be like grape clusters, and the scent of your breath like apples, and your kisses as exciting as the best of wine, smooth and sweet, causing the lips of those who are asleep to speak (Song of Sol. 7:1-9).

All those wonderful images are blessed by God within the bounds of marriage. Now, I don't have any tingling sensations when I think of Barb's nose as the tower of Lebanon or her eyes as the swimming pools in Heshbon, but there's just no way a woman could know how fascinating the female body is to a man.

Even some of my men friends disagree with my next statement, but it's one I want you to consider. I believe a man can notice a beautiful woman and simply appreciate God's design without lusting after her. As I've mentioned, I think it is IMPOSSIBLE for a man NOT to notice a beautiful woman. That's the way God designed him. We men just have to be careful in our noticing not to cross over into sin.

Barb and I drove across the mountains to visit one of my

favorite aunts who had cancer and was in a rest home. We made arrangements to meet my cousin Ray and his wife, Bev, at the rest home, and we were pleasantly surprised when my uncle Ted and his wife, Mary, also met us there. We visited with our aunt for a while, and then the three couples went out for lunch. We were having a wonderful visit, and as usual the men's and women's conversations drifted in different directions, and we became oblivious to what our mates were saying. We had a table by the window. All of a sudden, my 70-plus-year-old uncle drew the attention of his two 60-plus-year-old nephews to a long-stemmed beauty across the street.

No, it wasn't a flower but a smashing young vision of loveliness in short-short shorts and cowboy boots. What a knockout! We enjoyed this gift from God until she passed on down the street. I don't know what was going on in the minds of my uncle and cousin; probably the same thing that was going on in mine: "Thank You, Lord, for making women so beautiful and stunning." Then we went on eating our soup without another thought of her until I sat down to write this portion of the book.

Does it offend you that we men would find enjoyment in observing God's handiwork? We are not dirty old men, nor did we sin with our minds as the dream walked by. We looked. We appreciated. And we went back to our soup. Please accept the way your husband and all the rest of us are wired without being threatened. Please don't criticize us for it. In fact, you could have some fun with it as you walk down the beach and ask your husband, "What did you think of the bikini that just went by?" He'll deny having noticed the bikini, but you know he did, and it's okay with God, and when you understand how men are constructed, it will be okay with you, too.

He's Got a One-Track Mind

If you feel that all your husband ever thinks about is sex, you're right. It does take up a great deal of his mental time, and he comes to you hoping you'll want to enjoy the experience as much as he does. However, what often happens is that you're tired, the kids have you shaking like a mass of Jell-O, your mother is giving you fits, and your monthly moods make you not suicidal but HOMICIDAL. You've accepted too many things to do at the church, your boss is impossible to work for, the house is a mess, and can you believe it, your husband wants to go to bed early. You give so much of yourself 24 hours a day, seven days a week, without complaint, and you're supposed to be available for sex every time your husband sees the boat ad in *Popular Mechanics*.

By the way, this is one of those areas of marriage where you can use your gift of negotiation and have some fun. Maybe you need the screen door fixed, something taken to the dump, a room painted, help with the kids, the dishes, the vacuuming, one of a thousand other things; all you have to do is make a deal that the minute he finishes what you need done, you'll jump into bed with him. He would be honored, flattered, and breathless. He will probably hammer his thumb as he fixes the screen door or run into a pole on the way to the dump, but it's worth it to him. Make a deal as often as you want and you will have the most perfectly maintained home in the universe. But if he doesn't fix the screen door and he's a klutz at painting, don't withhold sex from him. He still wants you and his best present is still you.

When a man gets married, he assumes he will have unlimited sexual opportunities with the woman he loves. Then all of a sudden, there are monthly cycles, pregnancies, fatigue, relationship problems, ignorance on his part of how to be a good lover, and boom—the couple goes six weeks without coming together. The man has a little pressure gauge, and when he goes very long without a sexual release, the gauge gets into the danger zone and *cartoons* will turn him on. Or he'll see that silver silhouette of a woman's body on the mud flap of the truck in front of him, and he'll want to go home, look you up, and do something about his urge.

Some of the problems about sex come from mutual ignorance about what the other person wants and needs out of this part of marriage. Men think it all comes naturally. And many of them are completely ignorant about what a woman needs. These men have no idea that a woman heats up slowly, like an iron, and then cools down slowly. You already know your husband is designed like a light bulb: On! Off! He's snoring before you've had a chance to get your mind off dinner. *Who was that masked man?* And when he doesn't satisfy you (mostly because of his ignorance), you're confused and hurt, and you may even feel used. Naturally, you will be more reluctant to try it again next time.

If your husband never touches you unless he wants to go to bed, you feel more like an object than like a person he loves. But he doesn't understand, and he wonders why you aren't more enthusiastic. Kevin Leman has said that sex begins in the kitchen, with a relationship. Most men don't know this. So both partners get on edge. The husband is afraid to get too huggy and romantic because he worries that his wife will think he wants to go to bed. The wife is afraid to get too huggy and romantic because she's afraid that *will* give him a good idea.

On one of the survey responses I conducted in preparation for writing this book, a wife asked how her husband could have a big fight with her and then think going to bed would solve everything. Or how, having had a wonderful time in bed, he can get into a big fight with his wife not long after. This is simply more proof that men look at sex as an event and women look at it as part of a relationship.

Have Some Fun!

To help in this area, first remember that sex with you is the most fun thing your husband does, and you already know it can be fun for you, as well. It isn't that you don't enjoy sex, it is just that many other things distract you. Why not try being available to him more often simply because you love him? If I were a wife and knew what brought my husband his greatest joy, I would think of some creative ways to have him experience that joy as often as I could. We men get turned off pretty easily, and when it is obvious our wives are not as interested in the sexual part of marriage as we are, we find our joy in other areas like work or hobbies, or if a husband is not a Christian, he can begin to find joy in a new relationship.

Look at having sex as giving him a gift, because that's *exactly* how he will feel. Take your husband on as a project. Keep him off balance. Tease him. Flirt with him. Take the initiative in lovemaking once in a while. Surprise him and you'll have a very happy husband.

There are a number of wonderful books on the how-tos of married love that you and your husband can read together. Although it is not a new book, one of the best is Ed Wheat's *Intended for Pleasure.* Ignorance of what the other person needs is a major stumbling block preventing the sexual part of marriage from becoming all it can be.

God has clearly stated the rules with regard to husbands and wives:

> The man should give his wife all that is her right as a married woman, and the wife should do the same for her husband; for a girl who marries no longer has full right to her own body, for her husband then has his rights to it, too; and in the same way the husband no longer has full right to his own body, for it belongs also to his wife. So do not refuse these rights to each other. The only exception to this rule would be the agreement of both husband and wife to refrain from the rights of marriage for a limited time, so that they can give themselves more completely to prayer. Afterwards, they should come together again so that Satan won't be able to tempt them because of their lack of self-control (1 Cor. 7:3-5).

It's interesting to look up the Greek meaning of "come together again" in the above passage. The Greek word is *Hupotasso-Whoopee!* meaning three or more times a week. Now, don't blame me, ladies. Look up the Greek for yourself. Or you can ask Barb. On second thought, let's not bother her. Just trust me.

I remember one time Barb and I were scheduled to do separate conferences for the men and women of a particular church. The women's conference was first, and we had a great turnout. My last words to the women before adjourning were a request that they jump in bed with their husbands more often. The leader of the group picked up my line of reasoning and said she agreed this would be a good thing for the women to do, and they had four weeks before the men's conference to get things started. I guess the women followed instructions pretty well, because I'm told the men's sign-up was the largest in the church's history.

We did a follow-up conference the next year for both men and women, and after the first session, a young couple came up holding a baby and said, "Thanks a lot!"

So, just once before your husband dies, send the kids to stay overnight with their grandparents, cook your husband's favorite meal, light some candles, wear something that doesn't completely hide everything, and then let nature take its course and delight in each other. Yes, I know you sometimes meet him in your nightgown, but it has *feet* in it. You have to be more creative than that! Meet him at the door after work with nothing on sometime. (Just make sure it's not the UPS man.) I can't describe what a thrill it would be for him to know you can have some fun, too. But do this only once or twice in your husband's lifetime. His heart simply won't be able to stand the strain if you try it more often. And be sure to remember the byword, ladies: *Hupotasso-Whoopee!*

Now let's take a look at what a good sexual relationship can bring us—babies!

4

How to Parent Perfect Children: Just Ask Grandma and Grandpa

When Barb and I got married, there were no books on marriage or parenting. In fact, we had no idea how babies were started. I thought maybe she had to walk through a daffodil field and get pollinated or something. We wanted to start a family right away. About a month after our wedding Barb got sick, and she wanted to eat only crackers and pickles—before she got up in the morning. She also seemed to be putting on a little weight around the midsection, so she went to the doctor to see about a diet. Presto! She found out she was pregnant. Tim was on the way. He wasn't necessarily planned, but he wasn't *unplanned* either. Babies just "happened" way back in the olden days.

Barb was so cute in her little smocks. She was five months

along when we had to report to Fort Monmouth in New Jersey for army duty. So we packed our '55 Chevy to the roof and took off. Because Barb was pregnant, we got to know just about every service station owner across the 3,000 miles we traveled. It was summer, and they hadn't invented air conditioners yet, so Barb kept a wet towel around her to help her survive the heat. The '55 Chevy was in need of shocks, in addition to all the other discomforts, so she and Tim were bounced around a bit. She went through so much. And I wasn't even aware of her suffering. I just knew we had to get to the East Coast to join the army.

We finally arrived, but we were a little insecure being so far from home for the first time. As soon as we located the apartment where we would be living, we went out for dinner. I was alarmed by what we found there. The entire restaurant was filled with Mafia gangsters who were plotting murder and mayhem in small groups! I had seen people who looked like them in the movies and remembered what they did to newcomers muscling in on their territory. I tried to be cool so they wouldn't bump us off, break our legs, or threaten our grandmothers. Fortunately, they didn't seem to notice us, so we escaped unharmed.

As I thought about this adventure later, I realized we had never seen groups of Italian people in one place except in gangster movies. Neither Barb nor I had been east of Coeur d'Alene, Idaho, before, so we had much to learn about the sophisticated East Coast. All we had out west were Native Americans, covered wagons, and gold miners. The men in the restaurant that night were probably the local Baptist ministerial association having a Wednesday night Bible study. No wonder they didn't break my legs or threaten my grandmother! They were just plain human folks like us.

Barb went through 30 hours of labor with Tim, but he finally arrived. Husbands weren't allowed to go through the birthing process with their wives in those ancient times, so I spent a good portion of the time asleep in the waiting room. Today, of course, birth is a media event with cameras and concessions, but then I was helpless until the nurse walked in and said, "It's a boy."

I had no idea what that really meant. In our generation, we didn't do any getting ready for parenthood other than paint the baby's room pink or blue. We had no one to teach us what having a baby really meant in the way of time or resources. So after the "it's a boy" announcement, all I knew was to take my newly expanded family to our home and get back to work.

There's a biblical principle that states a man should not become involved in a new baby's life until the child is about six months old and starts to smile and becomes a "people." The *woman* is the one who has the God-given skills to take care of a newborn baby's needs, especially if they require getting up at night. I'm too busy writing this book right now to find the verse for you, but I know it's somewhere in the Bible if you'll just look for it.

Getting up at night involves another principle called the renticular activating system. This is the process whereby the brain filters out what we don't want to hear. We *choose* what we want to hear and ignore the rest. People who live near railroad tracks never hear the train. People living near the airport never hear the planes flying through the bathroom. And fathers of newborns never hear them crying at night.

Barb and I teach a Bible study to a group of couples associated with the Seattle Mariners baseball team, and I also do baseball chapels at the Kingdome. The players become our "kids" because we're old enough to be their parents. We have the privilege of helping them through some growing times when children come along, as well as in their relationships with each other and with coaches and fans. A few years ago, 16 babies were born to the players' wives and various other members of the Mariners organization in a short period of time. Believe me, it caused some stress!

Part of the stress came from the wives not realizing God's plan. It was obvious that since the players didn't get home from night games until after midnight, the babies, with their baseball genes, would sleep in until 10:00 A.M. at least, right? Not so. Some of the babies were up at 4:30 A.M., if you can believe that? That caused all sorts of disturbance. So I made a suggestion that didn't go over very well, though I thought it made perfect sense. I suggested the wives go live with their mothers for the first five or six months of the baby's life, since men were not designed to get up in the middle of the night, to be spit up on, or to change dirty diapers.

We're just not good at such things. We can hit a baseball traveling over 90 miles an hour, hit a little round white ball with a flat club 250 yards, and know which card in the computer has the printer interface. But dirty diapers are much too complicated for us to comprehend. Therefore, God asks the mother to be responsible for all this until the baby starts to get in control of things. I know you can see the wisdom of all this, and I'm surprised I get so much flak from women over such a simple principle.

Barb nursed our kids, which is God's wonderful plan for the newborn. I remember that it was my assignment to stay awake and visit with her during this special time. I don't think I ever made it. What I enjoyed was playing with Tim in creative ways, like dressing him up in army clothes. We also played "football" with him when he was just learning to walk. Barb and I would sit on the floor facing each other, and one of us would start him out. When he fell, that was the new scrimmage line, and we began the next series from there until he scored a goal.

I always had a shop in our home, no matter how small the house was. We couldn't afford new furniture, so we shopped at the local thrift and Goodwill stores, and I would fix up all the treasures we found. During Tim's early years, the only place I could have my shop was in his bedroom. We'd put him to bed after dinner, and then I would go into my "shop" to get something. He would stand at the rail of his bed and watch me. I would leave, and he would go back to sleep. Then I would need something else, and he would wake and stand up again.

I was so thickheaded. I had no idea I was disturbing a

precious little one's sleep. I had a goal—to fix our furniture—and the only time I had to work on it was in the evening. It was child abuse, pure and simple. (Tim, you knew there was something in your past that was nagging at you, didn't you? Now you can relax knowing what it was.)

During the last year I was in the army, Barb had a miscarriage, and we decided to wait until we got out of the service to start another baby. But—pass the crackers and pickles; Barb got herself pregnant again. At least that's how I remember it. She went home to Washington 55 days early because she couldn't fly too close to the birth date, and Bev was due the day I was to get out of the army. I know it was 55 days because I counted every one. It was so lonely without Barb and Tim, I didn't think I was going to make it. That period of my life is a little blurry because it was so sad.

Finally, Mr. Bekins came to transport our things. I had a few days leave coming so I started the drive home. I drove long hours so I could see my sweetheart and little son again. After some grueling days on the highway, I finally drove up the road to Barb's folks' home in Wenatchee, and we were a family once more.

Because Barb was ready to give birth to Bev, the doctor induced her labor on my last day in the service. So we had two babies compliments of the army. Tim cost us $7.50 and Bev cost $25, but everyone knows girls are more complicated than boys. Thanks, taxpayers. I really appreciate your kindnesses to us.

On the other hand, it was no more than we deserved since between September 1955 and September 1957, not *one* Russian Mig violated United States' airspace. Not *one* Soviet submarine was sighted coming up the Mississippi River. Not *one* atomic bomb leveled New York. I felt I had done my job of protecting Americans very well.

We had so much fun with our kids. When I was at the Salvation Army, Goodwill, and Saint Vincent DePaul looking for furniture treasures, I also picked up wagons and trikes and other toys I could fix for the kids. That was all we could afford, but I didn't even notice that we were what today's young couples would call "poor." We played golf on the lawn, slid down an old, used playground slide into a small swimming pool, went camping, and did lots of other family things.

Barb worked hard and was the best mother God ever invented, except she couldn't spell very well. When the kids were quite young, we'd all be in the car on the way home from church, and I would spell to Barb, "L-e-t-s s-t-o-p f-o-r i-c-e c-r-e-a-m." The kids would be jumping up and down in the back-seat yelling, "Ice cream! Ice cream!" and Barb would look over at me and say, "Run that by me again."

I remember all the typical trials and traumas of raising kids, like working for 20 minutes getting them into their snowsuits, and then they wanted to come back into the house after only one or two chilly minutes outside.

Beverly was a joy to raise. Barb and I felt that if God ever wanted another Mary, He would choose Bev. But I guess she wasn't completely perfect. After she was older she told us of some things she did—like dragging her hair in the street gutter so she would appear drowned since we were so insensitive as to suggest she could walk home from school in the rain.

Barb and I were worried that we had ruined Bev in terms of marriage. Because of our ministry, 90 percent of the couples who came into our lives were in trouble. I remember Bev saying one time, when the subject of marriage came up, "Who needs it?" Then a good-looking young man showed up in the front row of the Precept Bible Study she was teaching and they were married and now have given us the Two Most Perfect Grandsons in the universe.

Tim was another matter. He was a right-brain creative child—a Concrete Random (CR) learning style that I will describe in chapter 9. He had two main problems. The first one was that his parents didn't know anything about learning styles, and second, most schools are based on left brain subjects like science, reading, arithmetic, biology, chemistry, and so on. Right-brain subjects like art and music are shuffled into the if-you-can't-do-anything-else category.

As I look back, I know I failed Tim as he was growing up by not allowing him to be little the way my parents had allowed me to be little. Since he was the firstborn, I always considered him more grown up than he really was. (By the way, Tim has given me permission to tell you these things. He hopes his experience might help you deal with a creative child.)

Part of Tim's problem was that he had a perfect sister. That was because Bev, as the second child, simply observed the things Tim did to get in trouble and avoided them. I remember one time when Tim and Bev were toddlers, we heard Bev crying and fussing in the bedroom. As usual we called out, "Tim, stop hitting your sister." But the ruckus continued, so we dropped what we were doing and went to the bedroom, only to find Bev pounding her fists into Tim and yelling at the top of her voice. We probably punished Tim in error many times, and we feel bad about having been so ignorant.

When he was about 10, Tim stole a toy airplane from Mr. Savin's store in our neighborhood. After we found out about it, we made him go back to the store, ask Mr. Savin's forgiveness, and pay him for the plane. I'm sure that was one of the hardest things Tim ever did, but he grew from that experience, and I'm sure the owner was impressed, because he told him, "You're all right, Tim!"

Just *last night*, Tim and his wife, Tammie, called to tell us about the "thief" we had in the family—my four-year-old grandchild, Brooke. I was shocked. As far as I knew, Brooke was perfect and still is. I think they probably got one of the neighborhood girls mixed up with Brooke, and she is getting a bad rap. Anyway, according to the parents, Brooke had taken a can of pop from a locker at preschool. She made the mistake of telling her dad about it, and all of a sudden she was up to her neck in big trouble and got put to bed early.

Today she was scheduled to go to the school principal and ask her forgiveness. I should just stop writing and drive out there so she could have her "BaPa" to soothe her wounded spirit. However, when I suggested the idea to Barb, she said, "That's *all* she needs." I don't know what Barb meant by that. All I would do is cradle Brooke in my arms, and we would grieve together over the situation, then maybe go out for ice cream.

I just love grieving with Brooke. The more she cries, the more I sympathize, and soon she sounds like an old Model T truck that putts and putts. She tries to keep crying, but she has run out of tears. She needs to keep the emotion going, however, because her BaPa is doing such a good job of comforting her. Finally, we go to the sandbox and forget the whole thing. If anyone knows what Barb meant by her caustic statement, please drop me a note and fill me in. Anyway, when Tim talked to Barb about Brooke, he referred to his having to take back the toy airplane to Mr. Savin years before.

Tim was a dreamer, like most creative people. He would sit in class and all of a sudden wake up to the fact that the teacher had been talking for 15 minutes and he didn't have the foggiest notion what she had said. Tim's grades reflected his dreaming, too.

About the seventh grade or so, Tim began removing himself from family activities. We didn't realize it at the time, but part of his withdrawal was due to his beginning to smoke, and he wanted to hide it. I really violated the biblical principle of living in understanding with my family. I had no one in my life, including the pastor and teachers at church, who could make the Bible real. Therefore, I had no idea what the Bible said about child raising. I didn't realize I needed to invest time in getting to know how Tim was put together.

In junior high, Tim started having some hassles with his mom, and I took up an offense for Barb and emotionally cut off any meaningful relationship with him. Later on, Bill Gothard taught me what had happened. When someone we love is going through a conflict with another person, God gives our loved one the grace to go through the problem, but He doesn't do that for us. We're just onlookers at that point. If we get all tied up in knots about what's happening to the other person, and then the conflict gets solved, *we're* still left with the problem. We haven't been released.

In hindsight, I should have expressed my sadness and displeasure at Tim's decision to start smoking. I should have expressed my sadness and displeasure at how Tim was treating his mom. But I should have maintained an open relationship with him. I should not have based my love on his performance. I really failed him, and I have asked his forgiveness for my stupidity. I had no idea how to discipline, so I just punished.

Another way I failed Tim was not to allow him to have feelings, the same problem I've had with Barb. I hate conflict. When someone raises his voice or expresses negative feelings, I want the person to be quiet or I want to walk away. I hate confrontation with every fiber of my being. Yet over the years, learning how to handle it has helped me grow as a person. When Tim would express anger, I would tell him to be quiet, to go to his room, or to quit talking to his mother like that. I made no effort to find out what was bugging him. I saw symptoms that something was wrong, but I had no idea what the root problems might be. I could never fight my way through feelings of anger at his behavior to get to that real cause.

We had a power struggle every time it was Tim's turn to do the dinner dishes. He would sometimes still be doing them at ten o'clock at night. I don't know how he passed the time, except he did rig a complicated speaker and headphone system so he could listen to his tapes or the radio while he was "slaving" away. Our whole evening was consumed with the struggle of keeping him on the job.

As Tim approached 18 years of age, Barb and I decided to release him to God and let Him put the pressure on Tim if He wanted to change some of his habits and lifestyle. We had done all we could. So we told Tim he was now responsible to God, not us. We would always be his parents. Our home would always be his home. We would help whenever he wanted our help, but we would no longer dictate the kind of companions he should choose; he would have to make his own rule about when to come in; and he'd have to set his own lifestyle.

Believe it or not, all of a sudden, he was calling us at 3:00

A.M. and saying, "Don't worry, I'm just over here at Rob's." We weren't worrying; we were asleep. We knew God was watching out for him. It wasn't long before Tim was home at midnight, then in bed by 10:30, and soon in diesel school getting straight As. Releasing Tim to God brought him back to the family.

Today Tim says he can look back on his upbringing with understanding rather than bitterness. In fact, I got a note from him recently, reminding me once again that he felt I did what I thought best in raising him. Now that he's a father, I think he has still more understanding.

I'll write a book on parenting someday, but for now let me give you a couple of hints. Trust was one of the battlegrounds for Tim and me. He would get in trouble and say, "You don't trust me." I would reply, "You betcham, Red Rider, because you are not trustworthy." "But you don't trust me." "That's right, because you're not trustworthy."

Do you know what I should have done? I should have broken the cycle of mistrust. I should have trusted one more time, even though the chances were good that I would be burned again.

We parents get so excited when our teenager finally exhibits some responsibility. We in effect dust our hands and say, "Great! That's finished." Then he does some dumb, irresponsible thing, and we say, "What happened? I thought he was responsible now." We have to remember that he is an adult child. One minute he is responsible; the next he's not. My suggestion is to be sure to praise him when he is responsible and grieve with him when he makes a mistake.

After a while kids grow up and then they give you the World's Most Perfect Grandchildren. The World's Four Most Perfect Grandchildren so far are named Kjersten, Brooke, Cameron, and Connor. That means yours is number five at best. Don't blame me for this; I have no idea why God didn't give one of the Most Perfect Grandchildren to someone in Kansas or Romania or Edmonton. We are not to question the mind of God. If He decided to give one family the Four Most Perfect

Grandchildren, who are we to second-guess His purposes?

My job as a grandpa is to sprinkle stardust in my grandchildren's lives. It's the job of their *parents* to make them into useful citizens. Parents say to kids, "Be careful." Grandparents say to kids, "You didn't mean to." I've been accused of spoiling my grandchildren, but nothing could be further from the truth. As a grandfather, I have some definite rules that are absolutely nonnegotiable. They are steely cold, nonbending rules. In case you need to be more firm with *your* grandchildren, here are some of my rules for you to consider:

1. No hang gliding.
2. No jumping out of tall buildings.
3. No running across the I-5 freeway.
4. No playing on the Sea-Tac Airport runways.
5. Only 19 Popsicles in a row.

One thing they *are* allowed to do is chew a whole pack of gum at one time. Why not? Is it a sin or something? Should we save some of the pieces for the starving kids in Africa? We're going to chew the whole pack sometime anyway, so why not now? But if you enforce ridiculous rules like "One stick of gum at a time," here are some more for you:

1. Don't eat so much candy. Your teeth will rot.
2. You can't have a BB gun. You'll shoot your eye out.
3. Don't cross your eyes. They will freeze that way.
4. Don't wear your father's glasses. You'll go blind.
5. Wear clean shorts in case you get into an accident.
6. Chew each bite 37 times.
7. It will never get well if you pick at it.
8. A little fresh air won't kill you.

I remember so well the good times we had when God began bringing us grandchildren. Kjersten was the first. She's impulsive and changeable, just like her grandfather, so we did lots of different things when she came to visit. After we chewed a whole pack of gum, we would play hide-and-seek in the car, and she would hide on the floor in the backseat. I never could find her until she squealed or something. I looked and looked. I always had some parking money in my ashtray, and she would empty it and put all the coins in her pocket. She has a sack full at home. Her parents plan to retire early.

We would also go to the sandbox. We had a set of dishes there, and we cooked "broccoli," had "pie and ice cream," and let the sand run through some funnels. Then we swung for a while and climbed on the ropes. Then we worked with her back-hand on the tennis court, where she hit every forty-seventh ball or so. Then we'd ride the little battery-powered motorcycle. She would stop to have me put some "gas" in it with my finger so she could keep going. Then we'd drive to Greenlake and feed the ducks. Sometimes she would take off on a boat dock, running for all she was worth toward the water. Just before she went airborne, I would gently grab her from behind, and we would giggle and laugh before she took off down the dock again. If she had been *my* child, of course, I would have put three life jackets on her, had her chained to a tree, and would have said 356 times, "Don't go near the water! Do you hear me, young lady?"

After fun on the dock, we would come home and have a peanut party. Just me, Kjersten, the dog, and the cat. The four of us would sit on the kitchen floor as I would shell a peanut for Kjersten, then one for the dog, then one for the cat, then one for me, and then back to Kjersten again. We made a big mess, but that's what brooms are for.

Then we rode the trike for a few minutes. Then we would go into the living room, tip over some chairs, spread some blankets on top, and play "tents." Then we would go downstairs, where the sound-activated fish was, and clap our hands to make it move. Then we washed the dishes. I got some clean ones out of the cupboard and steadied Kjersten as she stood on a stool "washing" them. It was real hard for her to remember not to squirt water toward the window with the spray hose, but what's a little water? Windows don't rust.

She was pretty well soaked after washing the dishes, so she would take a bath in the sink. She liked to make bubbles with the liquid hand soap, and we used more squirts than some of you naysayers would think necessary. I haven't found a Bible verse yet that says how many squirts is too much, so we used lots. Occasionally, I took shots from Barb, who wanted me to use "moderation." So we used *half* the bottle rather than the whole thing. That's moderation if I've ever heard of any. Then we dried off and read a few pages of a book, watched five minutes of a Disney movie, and dozed off in front of a warm fire in each other's arms. Then her folks would come to take her home, and I would go to bed. I always got reports later that Kjersten zonked out the minute she hit the car seat. It's not surprising we were both exhausted. We have the same genes, so it's no wonder we have the same bedtime habits.

I have been known to exaggerate slightly just once in a while when talking with my grandkids. I would tell Kjersten how I used to feed the dinosaurs back when I was in school. I told her I rode in covered wagons and flew to the moon. I asked her if she knew that cows lay eggs. She would look at Barb, and Barb would slowly shake her head "no."

Sometimes Barb would whisper to Kjersten, "BaPa is lying." One time Kjersten and I were having a picnic with McDonald burgers in the back of my van. I was telling her how thankful I was to the Lord that He made her just for me. She said she thought God had made her for her parents. I repeated the fact that the Lord made her just for me. Since Barb wasn't there, Kjersten stopped eating for a minute, looked up to the ceiling of the van, and said, "Lord, is he lying?"

Brooke is our Secondborn Perfect Granddaughter. She's so different from Kjersten. Brooke will color for an hour all by herself. She's a wonderful pretender, where Kjersten is a little less patient.

Brooke is five years old at this writing, and one of the fun things we do when I bring her to my house on a date is play store. I bought a couple of old phones from Goodwill at one dollar each, and we have a bunch of odds and ends that she "sells." I bought her a little cash register and a good supply of Monopoly money. She arranges all the goods on the table in the basement, and we're set to play.

I have to call the saleslady to make sure the store is open every time I want to shop. She closes up at the drop of a hat to arrange some of her things. I surely don't want to drive all the way from the clothes washer to the furnace and have her be closed, so I have to call. I ask whether she has any balloons, cap guns, candy, or play dishes for sale. Then I ask the price, and she has to cradle the phone under her chin the way she sees her mom do and punch all the buttons on the cash register to figure out how much it will cost me. Then she comes back on the phone and says, "That will be two." Two dollars? Cents? Hundred? I never ask. I just take my money, drive down by the furnace, and pay for whatever it was I needed.

One time I gave her real money. I was supposed to get some change, but she closed the store, and I never did get my dollar bill back. We play this by the hour. What a precious little treasure!

Brooke loves to go shopping at real stores. One time when she was about three years old, she was riding in the car with me, and I pulled out the little idea sheet I keep in my pocket. I wrote down an idea, and then put it back in my pocket. She asked if she could see it. She made a little scribble on the paper. I asked her what it said. She pretended she was reading and said, "Go shopping." So, we stopped at the next department store we came to and went shopping.

I always give her a budget, and she is so good to stick with it. Do you think $500 is too much? No, I don't give her that much. Her budget is usually $5, and she is such a good little shopper. We go up and down the toy aisles until we wear a furrow in the floor and she decides what she wants. Every once in a while she'll point to a $40 doll, and I'll say, "Sorry, too expensive." One time as we were heading for the store to shop, she said, "And don't say 'pensive!"

I just came back from a break, but I have tears in my eyes as I write these words. I had to say good-bye to my precious grandson Cameron, and I probably won't see him for another *week.* His little face is so troubled when he finds out he has to leave. All I can see as he and his mom drive away is the top of a precious little head with two little eyes that hurt.

Okay, I know a big group of you have no understanding of how I could feel sad about being gone from my grandson a whole *week.* You're called *parents.* You don't know how blessed you are to be chosen by God to spend 24 hours a day, seven days a week, 365 days a year with your kids. What a priceless privilege, and you don't appreciate it. I didn't either, fully, but now I have a second chance to do it right.

As proof that men and women are different from the womb, Cameron and I do different things from what I did with the girls at the same age. He is just over one year old and hasn't been around long enough to be contaminated by parenting, environment, or the culture. He's just designed differently.

When he comes to our house, we first climb into the wagon and go up to the swings. After swinging for a while, we play in the sand. I played in the sand with the girls, too, but now, rather than cooking dinner on our play stove, we move sand with dump trucks. His choice, not mine. Then we go back in the house, to my basement office, to type a letter on the electric typewriter. It does marvelous things and sounds great. He isn't satisfied with just typing, however, even though he does a wonderful job. He needs to get his little fingers into where the ribbon goes and where the paper comes up and check out all the doodads. Here he is just over a year old, and he's fascinated with knobs, buttons, switches—anything mechanical. Then we play some music on my keyboard.

Finally, we check out all the neat things in the toy drawer. Then we eat lunch and let Molly, our dog, lick all the spoons and dishes and jars during the meal. I lose track of who licked what last, but that's not a big deal. I've read where dogs' mouths are cleaner than humans' mouths anyway.

I was feeding Cameron some Cheerios on his high chair tray recently, and once in a while I would flip one or two off the tray to Molly. Barb was reading the morning paper at the table, and without looking up, she suggested I not do that. I asked her why. She looked up, didn't have a good answer, and smiled—which meant go ahead. Then Molly began standing up with her front feet on Cameron's high chair tray and taking some Cheerios. Cameron was enjoying this game immensely. Barb was still reading the paper and, without looking up, suggested I not let Molly do that. I asked why. She looked up, couldn't explain why not, and in effect said to go ahead. She had fallen into the parent trap again, where everything that is fun gets an automatic "no."

Just a few months ago, our daughter, Bev, gave us Connor, the World's Most Perfect Fourthborn Grandchild. He's starting to smile, and I'm about to begin my bonding, but I really don't have much to tell you about him since he's not a people yet. I'll have to bring you up to date in my next book.

I don't write all this to torture you grandparents who don't have your grandkids living nearby. I just want to remind you of the priceless, overwhelming joy of spending time with those precious little lives if you possibly can.

The Second Time Around

Do you know why I have so much fun being a grandfather? It's because I get a second chance to do things right. I was so busy being a parent to my own kids that I forgot to have fun sometimes. I was so concerned about making them into useful citizens that I forgot to listen. I gave solutions when they hurt. I forgot to do more things *their* way instead of thinking of myself, my plans, and my needs.

You know why I think God invented grandparents? They're the only people with *time,* and that's the bottom line of parenting. The problem is, young parents don't *have* time to be everything their kids need along with working on marriages, starting careers, taking care of in-law responsibilities, and meeting church and social obligations. Because men are more goal- and work-oriented, they don't always take the time to be loving, caring fathers. They're often exhausted after working all day and cannot easily get up out of their chairs and play ball, read a book, or help with homework. Good fathers *do* get up out of their chairs, but they often don't spend as much time with the kids as their wives think they should.

Since the woman is more into relationships, it's easier for her to notice when the kids have needs that aren't being met. When she tells her husband about this, he feels criticized and becomes defensive. When she points out that he's being too hard on the kids, not spending enough time with them, or doesn't understand their feelings enough, he will usually back off quietly. In effect he's saying, "Since I'm not doing things right, I'll just let you handle it," and he goes to work, sits in front of the TV set, or hunts with his friends. As he gets more criticism, he retreats even further. He feels he's not a member of the team, at least where the kids are concerned.

Some Good Ideas for Parenting

I don't care what our culture says about the joys of single parenting. Parenting is a job made for two. A son needs to feel caring, nurturing, unconditional love from his mom. He needs to learn how to compete in the world from his dad. A daughter needs to be protected and taken care of by her father. She needs godly advice and oneness of spirit with her mother as they both enjoy being women.

If you are having lots of conflicts with your husband about raising the kids, the place to start is for both of you to make a recommitment to your marriage team. I've read where much of a child's self-esteem comes from the relationship his or her *parents* have, not the relationship they have with the child.

I suggest the two of you begin reading every good book you can get your hands on concerning parenting. I've listed in the Resource section some books that have been helpful to me. For instance, Dr. Bruce Narramore's book *Help! I'm a Parent* is one of the best I've ever read. Something I learned from him is that *punishment* looks to the past, with revenge for bad behavior in mind, and is often given in anger. *Discipline*, on the other hand, looks to the future, with instruction and coaching in mind so things will be done right the next time, and is given in love.

I was also interested in the fact that the word *discipline* in the Bible comes from the same root word as *disciple*. In other words, we are to disciple our kids in the same way Christ dealt with His disciples. This means we're to parent with patience, kindness, tenderness, compassion, a listening ear, a forgiving spirit, and most important, *unconditional* love.

Dr. James Dobson's book *Hide and Seek* is another I recommend highly. The bottom line is that children are a gift from God and need lots of tender, loving care.

Grandparents, do anything necessary to be where your grandkids can see you more than every other Christmas. Sell the business; quit the church; move the barn. If you have kids living in various places, cash in the retirement funds, buy an RV, and spend at least a month or so in the vicinity of each of your kids and their families every year. Don't live *with* them. Just be in the vicinity so you have free access to the grandkids. And you parents, take advantage of this time yourselves. Your parents haven't come to see you anyway. Plan an out-of-town vacation and let them baby-sit your home and kids while you go to Hawaii, Tahiti, or a Big 6 Motel in Kansas City.

And parents, if the grandparents can't come to you, *you* sell the business, quit the job, quit the church, and locate somewhere near them. Grandparents provide such an essential ingredient to a child's life; it's called unconditional love. Most grandparents love their grandkids because they *breathe*, not because they do or don't do something.

I've been talking about the ideal, of course. For many of you, it's impossible to relocate. My suggestion in that case is that if you're older, adopt some young children in your church or neighborhood who have no grandparents. And parents, if your folks aren't nearby, adopt some grandparents from the church or neighborhood, and let them have a part in raising your precious kids. It's impossible for me to stress enough the importance of a grandparent's love and what it does to the self-image and confidence of a precious little one who feels completely approved of, unconditionally loved, and pampered just a little. Who of us wouldn't enjoy some of that once in a while?

Now let's take a look at how men deal with relationships other than those with their wives, children, and grandchildren.

Resolve Clicking Conflicts: Go with the One Who Has the Gift

Most men and women approach and value relationships very differently. Recently, I learned that the TV remote control unit has something to do with relationships. I thought everyone in our home agreed with the rule that says whoever gets to the TV room first controls the clicker. That's a pretty straightforward rule, it seems to me. However, as I found out, only one member of our team (me) had this understanding.

Barb and I had decided to watch the World Series together on a Sunday. I make my living in advertising by producing commercials, but I don't necessarily like to watch *other people's* commercials, so I zap, click, or whatever you call using the remote to change channels. I can watch the World Series, three football games, a car race, an archaeological dig, a hot new country video, and an alien movie all at the same time. Yes, it takes a certain gift. It's mentioned in the list of gifts in 2 Sampson 4:5-6. Sampson talks about some people having the gift of criticism, the gift of silence, the gift of being right, and the gift of zapping. (You do know I'm kidding, don't you? There is no book of Sampson.)

Barb doesn't have this gift. She has no feel for when to zap and when to stop. If you can imagine this, she will stop on two people sitting at a table talking; a little boy crying; an ambulance scene, a schoolroom setting, a lovers' quarrel, or a 150-year-old black-and-white movie that you can't see for the scratches.

Being the more gifted zapper, I know those are not worthwhile subjects, so I stop on important things like an alien attack on the space base, a battle scene from World War II, a football game, skydiving, or the latest swimwear fashions. Now, here I have to be very discreet. The speed of zapping has to be constant among all these important subjects. Barb accuses me of a slightly longer hesitation as I come across the swimwear fashions. I must be losing my edge with age, because a gifted zapper should be able to maintain a consistent pace without anyone noticing there might be a bit more interest in one subject over another. As I say, it relates to giftedness, and not everyone can do this.

Anyway, I guess the pressure had been building up, so on that particular Sunday, I thought I had control of the clicker because I had come into the TV room first. I clearly fulfilled all the requirements for chief clicker of the day. I was happily flitting around the 500 channels waiting for the World Series commercials to end, and Barb began to make comments like, "Go back one. Stop there. Let's watch part of the news. That looks interesting. Wait! Stop! Go back to the dog that's dying." It suddenly dawned on me that just having the clicker in my hand did *not* make me chief clicker. The other person sitting in the room had definite ideas about what programs to stop on. I had flashbacks then to the thousands of times this had happened in the past, and something snapped in my brain.

So, very kindly and carefully, with a Christlike attitude, I set the clicker by Barb's chair and began to read. She said my attitude *wasn't* good. I clearly remember being calm, controlled, and kind, however. It just seemed logical to me that whoever needed to be "right" about what programs to stop on should also physically man (or woman) the clicker. She told me later—get this—that she thought we were having a *relationship* doing the clicking together. I would never have thought it had anything to do with a relationship. It had everything to do with physical objects called a TV and a clicker. All I knew was that someone in the room needed to make the clicking decisions the most, and it appeared to be Barb. So I did what any loving husband would do: I gave her the clicker. She got up and huffed (my word) out of the room with hurt feelings.

Later, when we talked about it, Barb said I had forever destroyed the "fun" of doing the clicking together as a loving couple. "Never again" would we be able to click together. We had lost a precious relationship experience. That was all news to me.

Here's what was happening. I am the world's most goal-oriented man. I have a thousand projects going at any moment. I have projects in progress in my workshop, in the basement, in my audio studio, in my TV editing area, and in my computer room where I write. I also have a long list of things to do for Barb around the house like clean the gutters, paint the patio ceiling, bring in some fireplace wood, clean out the basement, vacuum the pool house, run to the store, and rub her neck. Barb has had a hard life, because every time she wants to do something involving relationships, it stops me from accomplishing some goal, and I'm afraid I complain. Therefore, she looked at our joint clicking as one of those rare parts of our friendship where we could do something together, and I messed her up. I'm so sorry I didn't get the complete picture.

We haven't had any clicker conflicts lately. I think it's because Barb has given up the right to be the clicker operator, make comments, or ask to watch anything. I would like to think it's because of my Christlike attitude that the clicker is more available to her. I don't grab it first, take it to the bathroom with me during commercials, or hide it under the pillow, but I finally admitted I had a problem.

I wasn't going to tell you about this part of my life, but you need to know the whole story. I'm in a clicker 12-step program. I go to this meeting where we all sit around in a circle and know each other by our first names only. We start by admitting we have a problem. Then we have to admit we've hurt other people with our clicking. Next we have to seek a higher power's help. I'm just about finished with the program, but the instructors warn us that we're only one click away from going over the edge again. They gave me the name of someone I can call if I feel the urge to click.

One time Barb and I were at spring training with the Seattle Mariners baseball team and had a nice hotel suite with two TV sets. One was in the living room, the other in the bedroom. I was watching aliens eat people when all of a sudden, the channel changed to someone dying of cancer. I would switch back, and then it would click by itself to a couple visiting down by the lake. I would switch back to the aliens, and it would change to a ballet. Then I noticed Barb. She had eased the door open behind me and was clicking over my shoulder.

Barb tells me, "It used to be fun, but now I just keep quiet." I'm sad about that, but maybe she'll forgive me one of these days and we can get on with having fun. I really blew it. But how was I to know a clicker was involved in a relationship?

Most of the men I know don't value relationships outside the family as much as women do unless the contact offers some tangible benefit or meaningful reason why we have to get together. That doesn't mean we don't like people. We just have lots of goals that have a higher priority than getting together with a bunch of people—especially people we don't know. There are some exceptions to this, of course, but most men seem to feel this way.

One time Barb's Bible study leaders were having an evening get-together, and she wanted me to go with her. I had no idea why I had to go. I didn't know anyone who would be there, I had lots to do, and I'm not in one of her study groups anyway, so nothing related to me. I'm not that outgoing, either, so it was doubly hard for me to think about talking to a bunch of strangers.

Fortunately, there were some kids in the home where the meeting was held, so I spent most of the evening with them, while Barb and the leaders talked about their program. Barb didn't understand why I didn't want to go. It was because all of my life goals completely stop when I take time for a social function. I know that's hard for you to understand, but that's the way most men feel. What we men *should* do, however, is go with a happy face because after God, *our wives* are our highest priority.

One of the problems with relationships is that they involve visiting. I'm not a good visitor. After I get through the football, baseball, and basketball scores, I'm out of things to talk about—unless, of course, someone wants to commit suicide or is contemplating a divorce. I can talk all day with people like that, trying to help them with the things I'm learning in my Bible study and from my experience. But I'm not gifted in small talk.

Even terrorists are now taking advantage of the fact that most men aren't into visiting as much as women are. Did you read in the paper recently what a terrorist group in Iraq does to break the spirit of its male prisoners? The torture takes place in a simulated front room that's set up in Baghdad. They have coffee tables and overstuffed chairs, pictures on the walls, and soft pillows. They march the prisoners into the room, bring in hot dog buns with no wieners and Coke with no ice, and make them VISIT. After about 15 to 20 minutes, the prisoners are screaming to be released and will tell their captors anything they want to know about the secret missile bases and flight schedules. It's a horrible thing to see. The Geneva convention has this diabolical torture under consideration to see if it violates the rules of war.

I remember one time I got into special trouble with Barb. It seemed as if we had been relationshiping all day, and I was eager to get on with my life. We were on our way home when she decided to stop by a relative's house for "just a few seconds," and that's a direct quote—well, at least as I remember it. When Barb was editing this portion of the book, she wrote on my rough draft, "You lie." So maybe she said "short time," "for just a few minutes," or "just stop by," all of which mean to me that we would be there for only a few seconds.

Anyway, I didn't sit down when we got there, nor did I take off my coat. I had already invested many hours of my precious life visiting with people that day, so I wanted to get my life started again and change the world in some way. But the "few seconds," "short time," "for just a few minutes," or "just stop by" stretched into an hour. Barb even took off *her* coat and sat down. I couldn't believe it! We were only stopping by for a . . . (whatever). How could she lie to me so easily? Therefore, I spent the entire time with my coat on, standing up, ready to go, which probably looked real stupid to the folks there.

I can see now how I hurt Barb, but that wasn't my intention. I felt Barb was not sensitive to my sacrificial investment of a significant portion of my life in visiting that day. She probably saw my refusal to sit down or take off my coat as an affront to her and the people there, but I don't think anyone else noticed. All I wanted to do was salvage just a few minutes of the day to do something *important*.

I sound like an insensitive beast, don't I, not wanting to be with people or sharing my life with our friends. But that's not it at all. Barb's and my tolerance levels are just different. I love the people we dropped by to visit. I enjoy my friends and want to be with them. But there comes a time when I need to begin my life again.

Barb thinks visiting might be hard for men because we don't share our lives deeply with each other. I don't agree. We share in great depth many important aspects of our lives, like the football game from last Sunday. We share our feelings about our local football team's mistake of going into a prevent defense

during the last couple of minutes of the game when an attack-
ing defense is what got us the lead! We go into great detail
about why the coach made a mistake by sticking with a 4-3
defense when it's obvious we needed more men on the line. We
also talk deeply about whether our favorite baseball team has a
shot at getting into the play-offs.

We share deep feelings about how we grieved when our
baseball coach went to his bullpen too quickly in last night's
game. It's obvious some of the kids can master a left-handed
hitter down and in, but the team had great strength on the right
side. We also visit about the draft position of the various NBA
teams and make our predictions on who is going to win the
Indy 500.

Furthermore, we share our lives deeply when we relive the
golf game we had recently. We marvel at the pin placement on
number six. Even if you made it there in three, it would take at
least two putts to finish, and if you hit it long, you're in the
sand. So please don't ever accuse us men of not sharing our lives
deeply or enjoying the details of life.

Just reviewing our conversation above will show you how
easily we socialize and enjoy talking with our friends. However,
there comes a time when we need to move on. And at that
point our wives have barely gotten a good start on their fellowship. They've covered all the new babies and how much they
weighed and how long they were and whether they were having
problems nursing. They've talked about the husbands and how
they will never understand what he was thinking about when
. . . They've shared something they learned at Bible study last
week and how exciting it was to find out the verb was in the
Aristotle first voice of the principal tense. They've talked about
in-laws, their latest find in shoes, and the trouble they had
shopping in the crowd at Nordstroms, and they've traded seven
recipes. The businesswomen have described how much they
like or dislike the boss or a coworker or why they deserve a raise,
and the grandmas have shown everyone the latest rolls of
grandchildren pictures.

After all the women have seen the pictures, they come to the room where the men are deeply sharing their lives and want to show *them* the pictures. If you've seen one grandchild, you've seen them all unless *you* happen to have a few, and then you have your *own* pictures of them playing in the mud, hang gliding, or climbing to the top of a tree. The husbands have covered all the important points of using the 4-3 defense and the other vital topics of the day, and they're ready to go home. Then the wives get upset because they "never" want to visit. The fact is, *we've been visiting for 15 hours*, and our brains are going to explode if we do it for even two more minutes.

Barb's taste in films is strange, too. She keeps dragging me to movies that are entirely about relationships. There isn't one alien or battle scene. The people just sit there and visit during the whole movie. One she took me to was called *The Joy Luck Club*. There were 500 women in the movie, and the camera zoomed in on every one and told her life story. Then when we had seen all their stories in great detail and the camera had made what I hoped was its final zoom, the 500 *daughters* of the women at the table came in, and the camera had to zoom in on each of those folks and tell her life story. For a two-week movie it wasn't bad, but I prefer them a bit shorter.

Barb loves stories where the mom gets cancer, the little boy gets lost in the woods, the dog gets run over, or the couple gets a divorce or loses a child. Anything with tears she adores. We were in the fourth quarter of a movie that had all these things and then some. As I remember, the mother was having a heart attack at the time when Barb leaned over to me and wondered if I had expected the mother to die. I replied something like, "It doesn't surprise me. We've had everything else." Barb started to snort and giggle and make noise and had to leave the theater.

It reminds me of the time Barb dragged me to my first symphony concert. Remember, my music is country, so I was a little out of my comfort zone. I made my way through a couple thousand people in tuxes and fancy dresses roaming around the lobby. We were ushered into our seats, and the first thing Barb said to me was "Sshhh." Sshhh? When we went to my country shows, people loved to visit prior to the first act, but it was obvious no one wanted to do that here. I scraped my foot on the floor and had eight people turn around and glare. I sniffed my nose, and the usher came over to see if maybe I should go out.

The orchestra played its first number. It wasn't half as bad as I thought it would be. I was pleased. Then I found out they were only tuning up and the program hadn't started yet. Barb asked me to just hold my breath until intermission. I was doing a good job of that when what appeared to be a man came out and starting fluting. I had never understood how a real man could flute, but there he was. Barb glanced over at me and lost it and started to giggle. After being pelted with programs and umbrellas, we decided the people wanted us to leave, so we did. I'm sorry Barb didn't get to hear an entire symphony. She should go again sometime. I know she would enjoy it. I'm pretty sure I'll be busy, but I'll leave the light on for her.

Now that I've offended all you symphony lovers, don't get your noses *too* high in the air. Think of all the times you've put down my country music. Barb doesn't think George Jones opens his mouth wide enough, and she says all my music sounds the same. I'm surprised that a woman of her upbringing could miss the tender nuances of melody that rapture the heart as the steel guitar wends its happy pianissimo into the forte.

By now I can imagine you think Barb sounds pretty perfect. Well, I hope this doesn't disappoint you too much, but she is *not* doing all she could do to promote togetherness with me. For instance, we can't go on our 25-mile survival hike until she picks out the color backpack she wants. We can't take the summer trip through Death Valley on a motorcycle because she hasn't decided whether we should get a Harley or a Honda. I have plans for an amusement park here in Seattle called "Chuckland," but she's holding it up because she can't decide whether to make jam in the morning (like Mrs. Knott did on the berry farm in California) and take tickets in the afternoon, or take tickets in the morning and make jam in the afternoon.

Until she makes these crucial decisions, our relationship activity is on hold, and I don't think that's healthy.

Men have no idea how important relationships are to women. Yes, we notice their tendency to value relationships, but we seem to think it doesn't affect us in any way. Why should we be involved if our wives want to go to a wedding? I had to be taught that since Barb is my highest priority next to my relationship with Jesus Christ, the wedding then becomes equal in importance with Barb, because I'm committed to meeting her needs. I want to be a part of her life. But for so many years, I just didn't know how.

There were some things I did right by chance. When the kids were small, Barb and I always did our best communicating after dinner. There were usually children's shows on TV between 6:00 and 7:00 in the evening. So after dinner, the kids would leave the table to watch TV, the dogs would hop up on my lap, and Barb and I would talk about the events of the day. This time with her fulfilled her need to visit. After we had done that, I was free to go to my workshop or do anything else that helped me accomplish some goals that evening. Barb could read a book or do whatever she wanted to do, also.

After we were through visiting, the kids would come back in the kitchen and wash the dishes. Barb was a wonderful family manager, wasn't she? Now that our family is raised, we still find dinner is the best time to visit, but today it's often at a restaurant. Even back then we would go out to a restaurant once in a while. But I could always tell if I hadn't taken Barb out often enough: In the restaurant, she would reach over and cut my meat for me.

Take a Priority Check

The principle we've been talking about is that most men's goals involve things, whereas women's goals tend to be more people-oriented. Of course, you women have goals, too, but it's my impression that most of the time they have to do with your home and relationships, even if you work in the marketplace.

Take an inventory of your goals and priorities and see whether this fits your situation.

You could be president of IBM and still have a concern about whether the house is clean or whether you have chili in the cupboard for your husband. You probably have a goal to spend some time visiting and sharing your life during lunch with someone at work. Or you contact a friend in the neighborhood or church group whom you haven't seen for a while. You're usually very concerned about paying attention to extended family like your parents or attending the big birthday party planned for your great-aunt. You also have goals to make sure the drapes are cleaned, to paint one of the bedrooms, or to redo the kitchen.

As men, our goals tend to revolve around doing things like going bowling or to a football game. When we go to lunch, it's usually to solve a business problem, get acquainted with a potential client, or have a meal before we play golf or tennis together. The tendency is for men's talk to center on what we're *doing*, while women talk more about their relationships and what they're *feeling*.

When Barb goes to church alone, she looks for a person she knows to sit with, because she wants to share the experience with someone. When I go to church alone, I just walk in and sit down. My goal is to attend church, and that's what I'm doing.

Not long ago, I decided to drive down to a small town south of Seattle to hear some of God's music—which is, of course, bluegrass. Since that's not Barb's music of choice, she stayed home. But she asked, "Who are you going to take with you?"

I was puzzled. Why would I take anyone with me? All I was going to do was sit in a seat and enjoy a musical experience. For the life of me, I couldn't see why I would need to take someone with me. I had a goal, and that was to enjoy some of God's music. I could have taken our son, Tim, because he also loves God's music, but he was busy that night.

I have a goal in mind when we start singing the nineteenth verse of the last hymn at the Sunday church service and it's to get out of there as quickly as possible and get on with my life. Barb has a goal to stay around and visit. We've compromised. I go out to the car and listen to Chuck Swindoll tapes or read a book while Barb catches up on her relationships.

On the other hand, when we go to a retreat to speak, you'd think I was a party animal. I go around from table to table or person to person to welcome folks and make them feel comfortable. I hate to see teachers just walk in, teach, and then leave without making some contact with the people who have been listening. Therefore, my table-hopping and talking with people in line while we're waiting for our dinner make it appear I'm very outgoing. It's a mirage, however. It just means I have a goal, and that is to touch people's lives by sharing part of my life with them. Also, I'm in control of the situation. When I'm at a party, wedding, anniversary celebration, or other social event where I'm *not* in charge, I'm uncomfortable just standing around and making small talk.

Because women tend to be more relationship-oriented, they have a harder time pulling up roots and moving to another area. A woman's roots go deeply into her family, friends, church, and community. She worries about making new friends, leaving her family, and not being able to see the kids grow up in her church. Where will she find another doctor? She loves the one she has now. And where will they go to church? What school will the kids go to, and will it be as good as the one they now attend? How will she keep in contact with the friends she's leaving behind?

On the other hand, a man is interested in his new job and how it will advance his career. Besides, he feels he's taking the most important people along anyway—his wife and children—so he can just pick up and go.

Barb and I have many friends on the various sports teams around the United States, and we believe baseball is probably the hardest on family life. In football, the men go away for the weekend and then come home. In baseball, the players may be on the road for up to 15 or 16 days at a time. Because they spend so much time without their husbands, the baseball wives plan many activities together, and their friendships become very close. The men have a goal, and that's to play baseball. The women have a goal, too, and that's to form intimate relationships that will get them through the days until their most important relationship comes home.

I don't think a woman appreciates just how much she messes up a man's goals sometimes. He'll be working in his workshop and realize he needs some screws or nails. He'll decide to make a super quick trip to the hardware store and get back—pronto, fast, instantly. Then he makes a big mistake; he mentions his plan to his wife. All of a sudden, he's stopping by the supermarket for milk, the cleaners to pick up some skirts, the garden shop for the bedding plants, and a friend's house across town to deliver a birthday present. Suddenly, his goals come to a screeching halt, and he'll be lucky if he gets back into his shop at all that day. I'm not sure how to analyze this except that maybe he doesn't feel that the milk, cleaners, bedding plants, and birthday present are as important as the goal of getting his supplies and resuming his projects. But you as a woman are innocent of any wrongdoing. You just assume that as long as your husband is out, he could save you a trip. You don't mean to mess up his goals.

A woman's relationship goals make a difference in the way she comes home from work, too. The woman can come in from the marketplace very tired, but within half an hour or so, she's ready to talk about her day. The man comes home tired, too, but he grabs his newspaper or flips on the TV and never feels like talking, or at least he says he needs some space to recover from his day. Or maybe the woman is a homemaker and wants some adult talk after a day of "Mama" and "More ice ceem, peez."

This business of "re-entry" on the part of the husband is critical. He thinks that if he sits down to visit and discuss his day, the whole evening will be taken up with talking. What actually happens, however, is that when he gives his wife some time to explore her day and describe his own, she releases him to do

something else fairly quickly. She just wants to be involved in
his world and doesn't appreciate it when she asks him, "How
did work go?" and he only says, "Fine."

Here's one of those times when I can't read a woman's mind,
so I might be off base some. I feel a man talking about HIS day
might be part of the discussion, but only a part. I think his main
goal should be to let his wife share HER life and activities with
him. I believe one of a man's greatest gifts to his wife is listening. I wonder if a wife's need to discuss the man's day is not so
much for information as it is to see if he cares enough to spend
time with her. When a man's only comment after a day's work
is "fine," I'm pretty sure a woman feels like he's saying, "You're
not important." The man's act of sharing his day says, "I love
you." I'm sorry we men don't do a better job of taking time for
you women.

I was explaining the re-entry principle to our son, Tim, who
manages a diesel shop. I told him his wife, Tammie, needed to be
a part of his world when he came home. He knew she wouldn't
be interested in diesel engines, however; she studied to be an
attorney before she became a mama. I agreed she wasn't a diesel
mechanic, but I suggested that the next time she asked, "How'd
work go?" he should say something like this: "Well, Tammie,
you know that 236 engine we've been working on. We dropped
the pan on that baby and found iron shavings. That, of course,
meant the bearings were shot. I had Charlie come take a look
because he's our bearing man, and while he was working on it,
he took off the head and noticed the valves on cylinders two
and four were burned. Grinding those delayed us several hours
getting the job done, but we etc., etc., etc."

Tim couldn't believe she would be interested in all that.

"Trust me," I said.

So he went into lots of detail the next time she asked how
his day had gone. He later reported in a note to me that
"Tammie showered me with kisses." She was so glad he valued
the relationship enough to share his world with her!

We were in Phoenix for a conference a few years ago, and we

had an hour to kill before the first meeting. I suggested to Barb that it would be a great time to talk. She said, "I think I'll read the paper." I took that as a great compliment. Evidently, we were up to date in the talking department, so she was free to read the paper. I had filled her talking needs for that particular day.

I assume one of the most difficult things for you to understand about your husband, your father, or brothers in your life is the fact that they just don't seem to value relationships the way you do. Some of them do, but most of them don't. You have to plead and tug and pull to get your husband to visit your mother. You have to threaten and cajole to get him to go to a wedding with you. It's not a matter of his not liking your mother or not loving the kids who are getting married. It's just that he has so many *goals* to accomplish that it's hard for him to work on "less important" things like being with people.

On the other hand, you may be married to a party animal. He *always* wants to be with people. He's dragging *you* to all sorts of social outings. My guess would be, however, that if your husband is one of these, he usually has a specific goal. He probably wants to accomplish something by going out: getting to know a new client, attending a golf association banquet, or getting together in a Bible study. But when *you* suggest having dinner with one of *your* women friends he has never met, I'll bet that most of the time he will think it's a waste of time.

Men must be taught to value relationships. I'm not sure you can do this. You're much too close to the situation. Gary Smalley was my "third party" who taught me how important relationships are to Barb. The books he has written with John Trent would be helpful tools in explaining the relationship issue to the man in your life.

Almost every situation deals with a relationship. A woman with grown kids still needs to see them once in a while. Grandmothers and mothers are extremely important to most women and need attention. Social activities at church or at work are significant to women most of the time, too. A man will never be able to meet all your relationship needs, so the women in your neighborhood, in your Bible study, or at coffee breaks where you work are essential to your mental well-being. When I'm doing marriage counseling with a couple, I often find that the woman has no one with whom to cry. Her husband is being a jerk, and she is lonely and hopeless. You women have God's gift of relationships, and I'm very excited when I see this beautiful gift in action, especially with people who hurt. On the other hand, the man is more of a warrior. He can do it "his own self." He can tie his own shoes, wash his own face, and fix his own car. He doesn't ask for directions when he's lost or admit he has problems of any kind; and he knows that big boys don't cry and you suck it up and play hurt. Just this week, I was going into a home improvement warehouse and noticed a man wrestling a large filing cabinet into the back of his pickup. I asked if he needed some help. He smiled and said, "Thanks anyway. I can make it." He would be showing a weakness if he admitted he needed some help. I understood.

A man needs a relationship with his wife and kids, but that's just about it unless he's the rare party animal we talked about. Men tend to be loners and do-it-yourselfers.

Feeding a Starved Relationship

I'm sure there are times when you are starved for a relationship with your husband. He doesn't know that you need to share your life with him and have him share his with you. He doesn't realize you've been working in the marketplace or communicating with kids all day and want some loving companionship. Here's where I think you can help. I often find that a woman is quiet when she has a need. She may build up a little wall of resentment bricks around herself, and may not want to face her husband's anger by bringing up a problem. At this point, you must say, "Can we talk?" Otherwise, because of your husband's ignorance, you could go years without your need for relationship being met. He can find all the self-esteem, approval, and satisfaction he needs at work. He has no idea you are relationally starving at home.

Since he's not sharing his life with you now, even a little time will seem like a lot. So you might set aside just 15 minutes after the kids go to bed when you can sit down and have your husband's full attention. He has to agree that these 15 minutes are for relationship building. He can't have the newspaper on his lap or the TV on. These are *your* 15 minutes, and they're precious. Refer to this book and say I suggested that he give you 15 minutes of undivided attention.

I know some of you are saying, "You mean I have to schedule time with the most important person in my life? Doesn't that mean he really doesn't care or value me?" No, it doesn't mean that. He loves you, and he cares about you. He just doesn't know about your need to share. Have a sweet and kind spirit as you explain your need for 15 minutes of visiting time, and ask if he would commit himself to that.

Unless you're living with a real beast, this will look like a goal he can handle, and he *does* want to communicate with you. Set a timer so he knows you're not tricking him. Abide by that time limit carefully. Even if you're in the middle of saying something when the bell goes off, say, "Oops, time's up. I'll finish this tomorrow night." I can't guarantee this, but what might happen is, he will want to continue talking *after* the timer goes off. He's enjoying it and will now begin to meet more of your relationship needs. You are exposing him to the richness of your relationship as you laugh, tease, and sometimes cry during this special time together.

I don't want to oversell this idea because some women could stand on their heads and it wouldn't motivate their self-centered, insensitive, harsh, angry, untaught husbands to meet any of their needs. If that's your case, all I can do is grieve with you, pray for you, and refer you to chapter 14, where I discuss what to do in that situation.

Setting a time limit fulfills needs of both partners—your need to visit and his need for some time by himself to accomplish his goals. The time commitment means you both have hope.

Now that you know your husband's focus is on goals, rather than on relationships, try not to expect instant approval or acceptance from him when you announce the wedding or graduation that will be taking place during an important Raiders-Cowboys game on Saturday. You see, he has to go through a grieving process. He thought his life was a bowl of cherries and full of opportunity and sunshine, and then you bring in some rain by announcing a relationship event. When you first tell him, he might react negatively, and that's okay. Let him, and he'll do the right thing when it gets right down to it. He'll honor you eventually. It's such a shock to his system to contemplate weddings and church socials that it takes some time to bring him to the point of accepting this setback in his life. Be patient. Just let him grieve for a while without condemnation, and he'll have the car warmed up and waiting at the appointed time.

Remember not to read anything personal into his initial reaction. You're still vital, wonderful, and precious in his sight. You're not the issue. He has just had a goal blocked, and he needs a few minutes to recover from the shock.

My suggestion is to keep in mind that valuing relationships does not come naturally to your husband or the other men in your life. They can learn to do better because they love you, but not because they're suddenly changed into relationship-oriented beings.

The home is another arena where God's designs for men and women come into conflict. Let's explore what happens and how we can learn to deal with this set of differences.

6

Amazing!
Someone Cleans
the Bathroom

Because my self-esteem is not tied to how our house looks, I sometimes don't get around to making repairs as quickly as Barb would like. And my to-do list grows in the strangest ways.

One day not long ago, Barb was in our bedroom, and when she leaned her head back to scratch an itch on her chin, she noticed a crack in the ceiling that had been caused by the most expensive chimney flashing repairs in the history of civilization. And all of a sudden, I had another entry on my home repairs list that I have had a hard time getting to since I'm writing this book.

The repairmen have put tar, glue, cement, duck feathers, foam, and gunnysacks next to the chimney, and the water still leaks through the roof and falls on the ceiling of our bedroom, which causes a little, tiny, itsy-bitsy spot that Barb notices when she scratches her chin. I've practically lived in that stupid attic looking for leaks. The house was built in 1938, so there are pipes, wires, and choking insulation, and I have to crawl over all that, plus beams and supports, while balancing a stupid flashlight whose batteries fail just as I get to the chimney. Then, in the pitch blackness of the attic, I feel my way back through the obstacle course as I'm called to the phone because some thoughtless person chose this exact time to want to talk about his suicide. Barb says I overstate things, but this is exactly how things are!

Also, Barb walks around with her shoes off. This habit has caused me no end of pain, especially when we were training our puppy. The puppy might make a little, teeny, tiny mistake on the dark brown rug in my office. First of all, she didn't mean to. And second, no one was going to notice it after it dried. Then Barb came down to tell me something, *squish squish* went her feet, and I spent the next half day with my power washer and vinegar getting every last atom of puppy off the rug.

There was also the time she went into our pool house, again without her shoes, and some dumb pipe had sprung a leak and the rug was damp. Okay, wet. Well, it was going to be summer soon, and it would all dry up. But no, I had to dry it. So I climbed up into my *garage* attic this time to look for some fans to blow the rug dry. Fortunately, that attic has no pipes or wires to worry about—just 40 years of marriage accumulation, behind which were the fans I needed to dry out the pool house.

Included in the accumulation was the fold-out diaper dryer we used in our first rented home way back before you were born, and our kids are now in their late thirties. I have no idea why we're hanging on to this. Barb and I don't plan to have any more kids. We're too busy. And our grandchildren use disposables, so their moms are not interested in our diaper dryer. Even Goodwill doesn't want our diaper dryer. It's still in the "junk" stage—not old enough to be an antique, though it's getting close. Yet for some reason I have failed to grasp, Barb wants to take the diaper dryer with us every time we move.

Then there's Edison's first blue canning kettle Barb used to can fruit and vegetables for the Civil War soldiers who came through town. We'd get the fruit and vegetables by going to her folks' family farm and bringing back 19 boxes of apples, tomatoes, peaches, corn, and apricots in the trunk of the car.

When we returned home, I would take the 19 boxes out of the trunk and stack them neatly in the garage. Then we would get busy with business and kids and the house, and six months later, I would put the fruit in the garbage can. I did this at some personal risk, because by then the green feelers on the peaches and apricots would be fully developed, and they would keep trying to choke me as I wrestled them to the garbage can. One day I suggested to Barb that I just take the fruit boxes out of the trunk and put them directly in the garbage. Why all the storage? Barb still thinks she might get to them sometime, however, and she doesn't want to "waste" fruit.

The reason this is stressful is that a true Snyder never makes two trips. I try to bring all 19 boxes of fruit or 15 bags of groceries in from the car at one time. This, too, has its dangers because of all the stuff Barb keeps on the steps to our kitchen. Someday I'm going to trip over some of those things, and Barb will be a widow. From her standpoint, she wonders why, during the week, I don't take the items with me on my way upstairs rather than trying to step over everything. Well, how do I know what the stuff is on the stairs for? Maybe she's just storing things there. It's not obvious that just because my way is blocked, I should take everything upstairs. Besides, sometimes my hands are already full with the 16 boxes I'm carrying to the kitchen, so it's impractical for her to suggest I do this.

Barb scratched her chin again recently and noticed the paint was chipped on the ceiling of our patio area. She washed her face and noticed her faucet was leaking, and we just had the plumber here a few months ago. She went into one of the bathrooms we seldom use and found another leaking faucet. She wandered by the pool filter to inspect her nasty sturshums and noticed it needed changing and the leaf filter on the pool sweep was plugged and a wheel had come off. While she was at it, she observed that the garbage bag I was storing outside my shop should be moved because we were having company, and my stacks of papers and books around my desk needed to be shoved neatly under the bed, also because of the company.

It would be simple to prevent this stress in my life. All Barb would need to do is just keep looking straight ahead and have her shoes on at all times. But no, she is into her home as a part of herself.

We used to have a red velvet chair in our home that caused a number of conflicts as I was learning this principle of how closely Barb was tied in to her home. The dog we had at the time, Muffit, loved to sit in the chair, tucked in alongside my leg. So she shed a bit of hair—no big deal. The dog was way more important than the chair. The problem was, Barb didn't think a hairy red chair adequately expressed who she was. I thought a chair was a chair was a chair. I found out the chair was *Barb*.

Your Home Is You

We men have no idea how closely your self-esteem is tied in to your home and how it reflects who you are even if you work in the marketplace. We men think a leaky faucet is just a leaky faucet, the gutters are just gutters, and the broken window is just a broken window. We have to be taught that *you* are leaking or stuffed up or broken.

We're not into details, so we don't realize that we make your work harder by expecting you to pick up after us. We don't even *notice* the messes we leave lying around. I guess our moms picked up after us when we were growing up, and we continue this expectation into marriage. Sometimes we fall into the trap of assuming that picking up the stuff that clutters a house is just part of your job as a wife and mother and don't think much about it. But Barb explained to me that a woman can't even *begin* her work in the home until she has picked up everything the rest of the family has left out.

An illustration of this came out of a seminar we did for a group of coaches and their wives. Barb asked the coaches how they would like to go out on the football field every day before practice and pick up their wives' slips, bras, pantyhose, and other whatnots before they could start work. Of course, everyone laughed, but Barb pointed out that is exactly what it's like for a woman when the family leaves things around the house for her to pick up. Use this word picture with *your* husband, and I'll bet he'll be more sensitive. If he's still a slob, have him call Barb, and she will explain all this to him again.

We men have no idea how much work you do to make your home presentable for company. I even got to the place where I didn't like to have anyone come over because Barb would be vacuuming for days, it seemed. She would also dust everything, ask me to clean up my areas, and make me shove my books under the bed. She would prepare her best dishes and clean up her sewing room. Why was she doing all this just because a couple hundred people were coming over?

As far as I was concerned, when we had a group in, all we had to do was zip down to our friendly supermarket and pick up some Mother's Cookies, put them on a plate, and we were in business. There was no need to do all that Third-World-War-Type baking and slaving, vacuuming and dusting, cleaning up desks, and so on. Besides, I didn't want to play games with our guests. They needed to see me just as I was—messy.

Why couldn't Barb loosen up a bit? It was almost as if she didn't want it to appear that anyone lived in the house. If that's what she wanted, we should just put up ropes the way they do in George Washington's home, and no one would mess up anything. Our guests could travel around the house, lean over the ropes, and say, "My, my, that must be where Chuck and Barb have breakfast," and "Look at how clean Chuck's bedroom is." If she used ropes, no sand granules would ever find their way onto the rug.

For years I was blind to the fact that prior to having company, Barb would go into my bathroom to straighten, add clean towels, and wipe down the sink. I didn't know she was doing that; I just knew the sink always looked nice when I went into the bathroom. I guess I assumed that was the way I had left it that morning. Barb asked me one day who I thought straightened up everything after I used the bathroom. I had no idea. I hadn't really thought about it.

Now that I know a clean bathroom is Barb, I try to wipe down the sink after I use it and hang the towel with the label turned in. I didn't mean to make extra work for her. I just didn't know what she needed, and a few micro specks on the sink are not going to get my attention as a big deal.

Because most men are not into the details of life or don't know how much of a woman's self-esteem is involved in her home, we're likely to put down a new rug and never get the molding finished around the outside; or hang wallpaper and never quite get the trim on; or knock out a wall and make her live with a gaping hole staring her in the face for weeks or even years. This is why a man can keep four junk cars in the backyard that he never has time to fix or, when a window is broken in the house, just put up plastic sheeting and hope the wind doesn't blow. This explains why a certain man I heard about who lives in Seattle, writes books, and whose last name begins with S would decide to refinish all the cupboard doors in the kitchen at once. He stripped them all, but then he got busy at work while his wife's cupboard insides were exposed to the world for a couple of months.

I have to thank Dr. James Dobson for helping me see the problem with my approach in his book called *What Wives Wish Their Husbands Knew About Women*.[1] He gave me the first inkling that the house was more than a house; the chair was more than a chair; the gutters were more than just gutters; and the half-painted recreation room was more than a room missing some paint. To my amazement, he taught me that the chair was *Barb*. The gutters were *Barb*. The unfinished recreation room was *Barb*. These were incredible thoughts, but they turned out to be true.

There Is a Way to Get His Help

When you're expecting company, I suggest you say to your husband before you start your cleanup, "I want to make sure you'll be proud of our home when the city of Tacoma comes over Saturday night, so I'll be doing some extra things to get ready. Don't worry about it. I'm glad to do them. And if you have time, it would help me a great deal if you would dust off the roof, hand wash the driveway, scrub all the leaves on the rosebush," and whatever else you need done. If you keep quiet, he will see you working hard and will assume you resent having to do all those unnecessary (from his standpoint) things just to have a few hundred people in. I had to learn that Mother's Cookies were not Barb.

Your husband *wants* to be a good partner and helper for you, but you can't assume that what's important to you is important to him. He is just not designed that way, and he'll never change until a third party comes along to help him reconstruct his thinking. You, after God, are his highest priority. Therefore, keeping the home shipshape to reflect your personality will make perfect sense to him once he knows the tie-in. But someone has to tell him about it.

Since your husband doesn't know what's important to you, here's a suggestion that works well around our home. We have two lists on the refrigerator. One has the heading "Barb's Goals," and one reads "Chuck's Goals." Actually, I don't have many goals for her since she anticipates my needs so well. But the principle here is that with such lists in place, *you* no longer have to remind your husband of what he hasn't done. The *list* does the reminding. And when he finds out that you're so tied in with the appearance and maintenance of the house, I'll bet he will get more things done for you.

This reminds me of a principle Deborah Tannen explained in her wonderful book *You Just Don't Understand.*[2] She pointed out that because of a man's fear of failure, every time a woman asks him to do something that isn't getting done, he takes it as nagging, and he will subconsciously put off doing it for another couple of weeks until it looks like it is HIS idea. Therefore, every time she brings it up, he puts it off. If you use the refrigerator list idea, the note does the reminding, not you, and he isn't as threatened.

Another principle to remember is that your husband is not going to notice all your hard work unless you tell him about it. Try not to say, "I'm getting sick and tired of cleaning up after you!" He didn't know you were doing it in the first place, so his defensive nature will kick in, and he'll get quiet. I suggest saying something like, "I think I've been taking something for granted. Forgive me for this. I like to have a clean bathroom for company, and I've been coming in after you leave in the morning and wiping down the sink and straightening the towels. You had no reason to know this because you never see me do it. I was just wondering if you would help me keep the bathroom neat. Here's where I put the rag for this purpose, and here's how I need the towel hung. Could you do this for me? I would really appreciate it." And then you give him a big hug, tell him how wonderful he is for helping you, and take him to bed. (Just a little reminder.)

If you do it this way, I'll bet you'll have the cleanest bathroom in town. All your husband has to know is that you *need* this done to feel good. Remember that to a man, a sink is a sink. He has no idea that the sink is you. So you have to help him recalibrate his thinking

One reason men don't notice things that need to be done around the house is that many of them aren't into the details of life, as I mentioned earlier. We tend to be big-picture folks. Let's see how this fact of life affects a marriage.

7

Asking for Directions Is a Sure Sign of Weakness

We've already discussed that men tend to be goal-oriented, and women tend to be relationship-oriented even when they work in the marketplace. There's another principle involving goals, and that is that men tend to see the goal, and women usually can see all the details on how to get to the goal.

I'm the world's master goal setter. I have goals for today, tomorrow, next week, and 100 years from now if I'm still around. Barb, like most women, is very practical, and she can see all the reasons why my goals won't work. In the past, when I would mention a goal, Barb would say strange things like, "Can we afford it?" "Where are you going to park it?" and "Don't you already have one?" When she asked such questions or commented on details I had forgotten, I felt as if she didn't have any confidence in me. I would then feel put down, and I would back off too soon. I needed to do a better job of filling her in on my reasoning without getting defensive.

The way we've worked this out is that I've asked Barb to just let me dream without adding too many details. When I reach for the phone to call the contractor, *then* she can give me her opinions.

We have a tennis court at our home, and right after we moved in, I wanted to put a cover over it. It rains a lot in the winter in Seattle, and I thought we could use it more if it was covered. Since Barb knew I wanted to dream without hearing all the reasons why my dream wouldn't work, she just let me talk and dream and talk and dream. She knew there was no way we could afford the cover, but more than that, she just didn't want to ruin the feel of the woods and the peacefulness of the setting with a steel building.

One day a client placed a big order, and all of a sudden I saw how we could afford the cover. I was very excited. Then Barb said, "There's something I haven't told you. I don't *want* a cover on the tennis court because it will look like a warehouse, it won't fit in with the woods," and so on.

I was amazed she hadn't said anything earlier, but then I remembered our agreement. Since I'm committed to the fact that Barb is in charge of the house, she can decide whether we cover the tennis court. I'm comfortable with that. It's part of my commitment. But even after all these years, she still hasn't had a change of heart about that cover. Think of all the extra exercise I would get if we had a cover! It would probably help me prevent a heart attack so Barb wouldn't have to sell the house to pay taxes and move to Skid Road. In fact, I feel a little faint right now, but maybe it will pass.

It's obvious that Barb is into details and I'm into goals, and it shows up most when we get into the car to go someplace. Usually, Barb will have the route all planned out in her mind; I just take off. I don't consciously know quite how I'm going to get to my destination, but if I've been there before, I can just feel my way. I have to admit that sometimes I start out for work when I should be going to church. I've been known to go north when our destination was south. I can almost *depend* on turning the wrong way. In fact, if Barb isn't in the car with me and I feel that left is the way I should go, I'll turn *right,* and most of the time that will be the correct choice.

When I'm looking for an address, I wind my way down some streets in the general vicinity of where I want to go, and eventually, I spot a landmark to guide me to my destination. The idea is to keep the car moving at all times. It is a sign of weakness to stop and ask someone where I am. Just the other day, I was driving up a road looking for a right turn. If I had looked at the map (which is also a sign of weakness for most men), I would have seen that the area on my right was a long greenbelt. I ended up driving many miles out of my way because I thought there would be a cross street at any time. In fact, there *should* have been one. I think I'll write a letter to the city street department. Who cares about the few spotted owls I would displace with the road? At least I wouldn't spend my sunset years wandering around because some environmentalist felt like putting a big greenbelt in my way to cut emissions or something.

On the other hand, when Barb is driving somewhere, she usually knows that she drives 3.2 miles and turns right at the Texaco station; goes 1.7 miles to the yellow sign that says "Willows Bluff" and turns left; continues until she sees the hotel sign; and then makes a left turn and she's there. Barb hates it when I'm lost and she has friends in the car and doesn't want to look as if she's telling me what to do. So she refrains from giving directions on those occasions.

We were in Hawaii one time and had some guests in the car with us, and I got into a horrible mess because Barb didn't do her job. All she had to do was offer a disclaimer, "Folks, Chuck has asked me to be the navigator when we're in the car, and it's my impression that we're going exactly opposite to the way we should be going. I suggest we do a U-turn as soon as it's convenient." You can use the same approach with your husband. I think I do pretty well when Barb is in the car, but she wonders how I make it to work when she's not with me.

Barb is the detail person in all the other areas of our married life, too. Not only does she notice the details, but she also needs to get them *right* for some reason. For a long time, I didn't know Barb had that need. I would be telling a story at dinner with some friends, and all of a sudden she would interrupt with a detail I had missed or gotten wrong. She would then add a couple of corrections and eventually take over the whole story as I sat there steaming inside. Who cares if my details were mixed up a bit? At least I got to the right point.

One time a woman who worked for us asked me about the sights to see in Twisp or maybe it was Winthrop, small towns in eastern Washington that Barb and I had visited. Small towns all look the same. Anyway, Barb was out shopping, and I couldn't ask her about it. So I suggested my friend and her husband eat in the local hotel because all the old miners in the community had breakfast there. They gathered around a big table, played cards, and told stories about the olden days, and it was fun to hear them banter back and forth.

When my helper got back from her vacation, she told Barb how much they regretted not having had time to eat in the hotel I had told them about. Barb said, "What hotel?" Well, I guess the hotel I was thinking of is in LaConner, which is about 175 miles from Twisp or Winthrop or whatever.

How could I remember a piddling detail like that? A small-town hotel is a small-town hotel. Miners are miners—only they turned out to be tulip farmers, according to Barb. Miners, farmers—they all wear greasy Caterpillar caps, so who cares what they do for a living? It was just not that important, at least to me. But it sure is important to Barb. She has this strange need to get the details right.

The way I learned to handle Barb's interruptions of my stories was to look at us as a baseball broadcast team. One announcer does the play-by-play. A second announcer does the color. The play-by-play announcer might report that the hitter smashed a hard grounder through the hole at short, and the color announcer would interrupt and say that the player was batting .314, leads the league in stolen bases, lives in California during the off-season, and enjoys pizza. Does the play-by-play announcer get all threatened when his partner interrupts? Does he say, "Would you shut up?" Not at all. He appreciates the help. So now when Barb and I take you out for dinner, just think of me as doing the play-by-play while Barb adds the color.

The principle to keep in mind here is that your husband really *can't* remember, and he really *isn't* lying. When you accept this, you can let him tell his stories any old way he wants. Usually no one at the table is going to know the difference anyway, and I've found that sometimes stories need a little over-stating just to make them funny. It's called artist's license. I'll have to admit that sometimes when I'm telling a story, I come to a dead end, forget my point, or wonder how I got to that subject, and then I *need* Barb to bail me out. In that case, when she takes over the story, I'm relieved and can sit back and relax.

One of the hardest things for a husband to survive is when he comes home and his wife says, "Notice anything different?" He's instantly in big trouble because he's missed something. So he might say, "Oh, you bought a new sofa. That's very pretty." ("No, we didn't get a new sofa.") "You had the place painted. I love the color." ("No, I didn't get the place painted, I got the drapes cleaned.") He didn't even know you *had* drapes, let alone whether they were dirty. And just because they had been at the cleaners for a few weeks, how was he to notice?

Another time when a wife says, "Notice anything different?" perhaps she has cleaned the cupboards, and now the cloves are next to the celery salt. Or maybe she got her hair done. The problem with Barb's haircuts is that her stylist cuts her hair with a microscope. He goes "a snippy snip here and a snippy snip there, and that will be $40, please." Her hair is one billionth of a millimeter shorter, and I'm supposed to notice!

Okay, wives, here's the solution. You must give your husband hints. "Notice anything different about my *hair?*" and "Don't you think the drapes look better *cleaned?*" He needs these hints badly to stay out of trouble.

Barb thinks that sometimes we men remember only what we want to. Way back in the olden days, I used to fix black-and-white TV sets to earn a little extra money. I knew which tube handled the audio, which was the high-voltage tube, and which one controlled the horizontal hold. I even knew the names and numbers by heart. But I couldn't for the life of me remember to put the plastic dishes in the *top* of the dishwasher or which way our daughter Beverly's dress went on.

Barb went to church early one Sunday when Bev was small and left her for me to dress. I got her dressed all right, but Barb had to redo things after we got to church. I thought buttons always went in front! And the reason she wasn't sliding down the slide very well was that I had forgotten to put panties on her. I had missed some details of life.

Something happened that demonstrated once again that I'm not as much into details as Barb is. A few years ago I lost my major advertising account because of a change in management. So I thought maybe the Lord wanted me to work more in writing, speaking with Barb at seminars, and teaching rather than just making money. Accordingly, we put our house on the market. It's a large home that we've used for entertaining, but without a large cash flow, we couldn't stay in it. It's a one-of-a-kind property five minutes from the heart of Seattle, with four acres of woods, tennis and sports courts, swimming pool, and other facilities for entertaining. I have kept the price fairly high because I feel that someday someone is going to come along and want the nicest piece of property in metro Seattle. There are no comparable homes, so it's worth whatever the buyer thinks it's worth.

I was resurfacing the courts and painting and cleaning and repairing the house to make sure it was in good shape for the person who bought it. One of the things I wanted to do was to power wash the driveway. We had been in the home for more than 16 years, and I had never cleared the moss and dirt out of the expansion cracks in the cement, so I decided that was something I should do.

I had gotten into trouble with Barb a few times in the past with my power washer. It does splash mud and leaves around, and I admit that the first time I used it, I didn't clean up as much as I should have. Therefore, Barb has never really trusted me with it. The truth is that since then, I have cleaned the moss off the patio quite a few times, and she hasn't even noticed. But I really blew it with the driveway.

It was August, and there were flowers of some kind—red ones with some white ones mixed in—lining the driveway. They looked like the flowers I had seen at our local hardware store last spring at five for a buck, so I didn't put a high value on them the way I should have. In fact, I hardly noticed they were there. I suppose subconsciously I thought that if I just happened to hurt a couple of the flowers with my power washer, we could replace them easily.

So I proceeded to wash the driveway, and it went great. You could eat off the cement, it was so clean. Then Barb came home a little earlier than I had planned, and I hadn't had a chance to clean up yet. She was shocked at the "devastation," as she described it. Upon closer inspection, I did find that I had gotten three millimeters of dust on a couple of the flowers (Barb would tell you they were covered with "mud," but I think she's being a little too sensitive), and she proceeded with great fervor to tell me how clean the driveway looked, "but I had destroyed everything else." Now, that was not an accurate statement. The garage, cars, and pool house were still standing, so I had not destroyed *everything*. I'll never figure out why women exaggerate so much.

Anyway, I was destroyed. Here I was working so hard to make our home presentable for sale, and I got in big trouble with Barb. In fact, I thought maybe our marriage was ended, it had that much emotion for her. Barb spent the next day or two dusting off the flowers. I had no idea that she had nurtured some of those flowers for *three years*, taking them out at the end of summer and putting them in the garage for the winter. And one of them was a direct descendant of the nasty sturshum that George Washington had taken with him to Valley Forge. At least it felt that important. I didn't really notice that the flowers might be in harm's way. I'm not into flowers, and one looks just like another except some of them are different colors, and they are on sale at the hardware store at five for a buck.

Obviously, flowers don't rank very high on my priority list. But since Barb does, I apologized for being so insensitive about the flowers, and she did forgive me, though it took a little while because she was so hurt. The bottom line was a difference in what we valued. Since I'm not into details, I valued sparkling-clean cement, and she valued flowers that I hardly noticed.

Women also tend to notice lint, hairs, or ketchup spots on the clothes we wear. I'll be walking out the door, and Barb will stop me as she expresses amazement that I haven't seen the Popsicle stains on my pants left over from the grandchildren's last visit.

There's something about this that troubles me a little. It'll take a moment to explain. I have never thought the theory of evolution made much sense. If it's a continuing process as the evolutionists say, then I need some mid-species samples walking around on their way to becoming something else. I need to see a half-whale, half-bird or half-dog, half-cat before I can accept a half-monkey, half-man. And for sure I need fossil records of this change between species more graphic than some partial skull dug up in Africa.

The evidence is not overwhelming, that's for sure—except for one thing. Have you ever been to the monkey house at the zoo? Have you noticed the mother monkey taking fleas and ticks and pieces of banana skin off the husband and children monkeys? It looks very much like what Barb does just before we go out somewhere. She takes something out of my ear, brushes some dog hair off my coat, chips some pizza topping off my tie, or adjusts the back of my hair. I don't know if this is a remnant of evolution, but it does have me a bit worried.

When Barb and I do a marriage conference just for women, they all come with their notepads and are even there a little early. They don't want to take any breaks. They groan when we have to stop for lunch. They don't want any free time. They only want to learn *all* the details of what we talk about.

When we speak just to men, however, we never get through all our material. Men are wired differently. They can sit only so long at retreats. They have basketball games planned at the breaks and during the noon hour. They need free time in the afternoon for volleyball and horseshoes. There's no way you as a woman would know this, but there's a nerve going from a man's behind to his brain. At about 28 minutes, a small alarm goes off in his head that tells him he's been sitting a long time.

Sometimes he is forced to reset the alarm because the pastor or seminar speaker is going more than 28 minutes. He does this by pulling his left earlobe and holding his breath for ten seconds. He doesn't get another 28 minutes, however. The alarm now goes off every *five* minutes. So, it's crucial to get your husband out of the seminar or preaching session as soon after the first alarm goes off as you can. His brain will explode if the alarm is set more than four times, so you can see how important it is that you know this fact of anatomy. Don't bother looking at the charts in the doctor's office; this particular nerve is hidden behind a bone, and not too many people know about it.

Perhaps He's Afraid

The reason a man resists when his wife questions his goals or adds details to his stories is that he feels like a two-year-old who has to be corrected all the time. He also feels as if he has failed again because he can't even tell a story right. I believe a man's greatest fear is the fear of failure, and that affects almost every area of his life. That's why he reacts so negatively when you tell him the pictures weren't hung low enough, he put the plastic in the wrong place in the dishwasher, he scraped the lawn when he mowed it, or he splattered when he painted the lawn chairs.

From your standpoint you assume that since he loves you

and is committed, he would appreciate knowing if he did the
job right. When you comment on things he did wrong he is
devastated. If he makes mistakes, it destroys his self-esteem.
What he really needs is approval and support. I think that's why
the Bible talks in Titus 2:4 about the wife loving her husband
with a *phileo* love. This kind of love means to have a fondness
for him, to be attracted to him so you will make fun for him and
with him. This love would make you want to flirt with him,
laugh with him, look into his eyes with admiration, and take
him to bed once in a while. Because you value him so highly,
you praise him, pay attention to him, and build him up. On the
other hand, husbands are told to love their wives with *agape*
love, which means we are asked to die for them. (More about
this later.)

Now I know that the focus of your heart is not to put your
husband down. You're just sure that he wants to get his stories
straight and that he would love to do things "right" because he's
committed to you. If you keep in mind his fear of failure, it will
explain his defensive nature most of the time. It will be your cue
to build him up and tell him how wonderful he is in other areas
of the marriage.

We've talked about how much a woman's self-esteem is
involved in her home and her need to get the details of life
correct. Now let's take a look at where a man gets *his* self-
esteem. This won't be news to you, but I hope it will give you
more understanding about how your husband's mind works.

8

His Other Love . . . Work

My work history starts on my grandfather's farm way back before you were born. As a nine-year-old, I began driving a wheat truck in the fields. My uncles had to put a mattress on the seat so I could see out the windshield. I would have to scoot down to reach the clutch pedal, so if you were watching me from the outside, you would see me disappear every time I shifted gears. I was also taught how to drive a tractor and do field work.

When I got in from the field, I milked the cows and fed the pigs, horses, and chickens. I gathered eggs, weeded the garden, and picked fruit. At the time, I thought *all* nine-year-olds had as much responsibility. I didn't look at all this as a big deal until later in life.

I made mistakes that caused my uncles grief from time to time. I remember one time doing some painting for my grandmother, including painting the seats in the outhouse. I did a beautiful job on them, but it didn't occur to me to post a "Wet Paint" sign. Just as I got finished and was putting away my paint in the garage, Uncle Clarence came in from the fields, sat down in the outhouse, and got branded. I remember looking out from behind a chair in the kitchen as my grandmother took paint thinner to my uncle's posterior. I'm sure it stung, and the paint thinner smell probably reminded him all day of what his stupid nephew had done, but he seemed to love me anyway.

I had a Red Rider BB gun and loved target shooting around the farm. One day I shot Charlie, one of my grandfather's prize hogs. Charlie grunted and died. I was terrified. There was no way I could explain myself when my grandfather found his dead pig. That evening, just before I gathered the courage to tell him about my awful deed, I saw him feeding the pigs, and there was Charlie munching along with the rest of them. Charlie probably thought the BB sting was some fly biting him and didn't even wake up. It was a good lesson, though, and from then on, the animals were safe.

After my farming years I attended Washington State College (now University). Way back in the olden days, every male had to put in two years of military service. I decided to go through ROTC so I could be an officer and not have to crawl around in the mud like the enlisted men had to do. I decided I would go into the air force—but the line of applicants stretched all around the college gym. Since there were only three guys in the army line, as I remember, I opted for the army. I know you understand that I saved at least an hour by not waiting for the air force line to go down. I had a busy life and had lots to do and couldn't be wasting my youth standing in line.

After I graduated, I went into the army and I suggested to them that I would do my best work if I were stationed near my hometown of Tacoma, Washington. Of course, the army decided I could really help them on the East Coast, just about as far away from home as I could get without getting on a ship and sailing into the Atlantic Ocean. I was assigned to the First Radio, TV, and Leaflet Battalion at the Psychological Warfare Center.

I can't even remember what I did those first few months, but soon a position opened up for me to serve as the public information officer for the PsyWar Center. I applied and got the job. What a difference! Rather than supervising enlisted men, picking up pine cones, or making new rake marks under the barracks, I almost had a real job. A couple of sergeants helped me, and I proceeded to make our PsyWar commander famous in the camp newspaper. I guess I did too good a job, because after six months or so I was sent back down to the battalion. I was told that the base commander didn't like one of his subordinates getting all the publicity.

So, I was made training officer for the battalion. I was a second lieutenant in a major's position. That brought all kinds of challenges, because here, all of a sudden, was a second lieutenant telling the company commanders what to do, and they were captains. It was one of my first learning experiences in being a servant. As I served the officers and the men in the battalion, they were not too concerned about giving me leadership.

Because of my "thoughtful" decision to go into army ROTC, it turned out I did get to play tennis with the colonel rather than doing push-ups with the enlisted men. And since I was in the Signal Corps, I knew where the AC plug-in was located on the power generator. So on field exercises, I could shave with my electric razor rather than the shave-in-cold-water-in-a-helmet-with-a-dull-bayonet routine. I was also able to live in officers' housing, which was much better than what enlisted people had. The officers' club where I could eat had wonderful meals and perks. I think that began my life philosophy which is, I believe it is much better to be rich and healthy than poor and sick.

After I had done my service to my country in the army, we went home to Washington state and we stayed with Barb's folks in Wenatchee. I packed apples in her uncle's warehouse. Once in a while we would drive over the mountains to see my parents in Tacoma, and one time while we were there, a Kit Spier called from KING-TV and wanted me to interview for a floor director's job. KING-TV was the top station in Seattle at that time, and I was thrilled to be considered. I was told that another man would be competing with me for the job, but I would take my chances. I painted sets, cued actors, set up props, worked on remotes, and was thrilled to be in the exciting world of television. I was so excited, I offered to do *extra* things. And when I had to work a little overtime, I didn't complain.

One of the worst jobs I had was working on a boxing show called "King's Ring." The station carpenter built a ring out of four-by-four logs (it seemed), and we had to drag all the logs, ropes, and tarps out of storage each week and set up the ring, then take it down again in one night. It was a real hassle. Among my duties was emptying the boxers' spit buckets, but I took that in stride with all my other assignments. I'm told, however, that the man competing with me for the job complained about working overtime, didn't do anything extra, and evidently refused to empty the spit buckets, so I got the job. I guess my spit-bucket work convinced them I was the better man.

I remember so clearly my first full day on the job after I had won the position. There I was, standing beside a TV camera with one of my idols a few feet away—Charles Herring. I couldn't believe that a farm boy from Coulee City would be working with the most popular newscaster in the Northwest. I was in shock for days. He treated me just like a PERSON.

All the shows and commercials were live in those days, and we had lots of adventures. One of my first assignments was to put an Alka-Seltzer tablet into Mr. Herring's water glass so it would be fizzing nicely when he held it up to go to the commercial during the news. The director would switch to a close-up lens, and I would crawl in on my hands and knees, reach up, and put the tablet in the glass. One time the director got busy and forgot to go to the close-up. I was new, so I didn't know a long lens from a short one, and I crawled in to do my duty— right in front of the entire Northwest. I didn't get fired; it wasn't my fault; but it did make for some fun memories.

I enjoyed the remotes we televised from various manufacturing plants around the area. One time my job was to cue a Japanese man to hoist a big fish out of a tank. I carefully explained what I wanted him to do, and he nodded and bowed. Then we went live. His turn came, and I cued him. He nodded and bowed. I cued him again. He nodded and bowed. I cued him again. He nodded and bowed. I found out later he didn't understand English, so we never did see the big fish in the tank.

Next I was made producer/director. That was a wonderful challenge. It was the type of job that needed specific gifts. You had to learn to take the pressure of doing a live show, instantly fixing things when they went wrong during the program; making sure the actors were ready for their cues; ensuring the right music was cued; seeing that the sets were in place; making certain the right commercials were on hand; and hitting the network on the second. I loved it. It fit my personality perfectly.

I especially loved directing the news, because we were always on the edge of disaster. At 30 seconds before airtime, someone would hand me a script I had never seen, the photographer would take the news film I had never seen to master control, and the news pictures I had never seen would be placed on an easel in the studio. Then at 6:30 P.M. sharp, we rolled the theme, and we were on the air.

I get excited about it all over again as I write these words, but it wasn't all good. I wasn't seeing my kids enough. Since the newscasts were in the evening, I went to work around 3:00 P.M., which was before the kids came home from school, and I got home around 1:00 A.M., which was long after they had gone to bed. I was still asleep when they left for school the next morning. So when a chance to direct some of the daytime shows came up, I took it, even though it wasn't as exciting or satisfying as directing the news.

After spending a few more years directing, I worked for a time making documentary films. Then a chance at middle management came up and I took it. My job as operations manager was to oversee everything that wasn't live in the studio. That included the networks, movies, commercials, announcers, station logs, and shipping department. I worked hard and enjoyed all my working relationships.

After three or four years, however, I noticed that my work never got done. The things I put in my "out" basket at night were in my "in" basket the next morning. The network would never do what it said it would. The movies never arrived on time. The commercial films would always break, and I felt as though I could have been working in a steel mill, because I had gotten out of live TV, which was my first love. I guess I was in line for a promotion to upper management at some point, but I didn't like what I saw in terms of the time commitment that would require. My boss came in early in the morning and stayed late at night. His boss did the same, and since having a relationship with my family was a higher priority than making money, I really felt God was calling me to move on.

After leaving the TV station, I began my job search by having lunch with the head of an advertising agency for whom I had produced commercials while I was a director. I had taken Advertising 101 at Washington State, so I assumed that was enough background to look for a job in the field. I asked him if he knew anyone in town who needed some help. He said he didn't know of anyone else, but *he* needed some help, so I went to work for him.

My primary job was to write and produce commercials for a supermarket. I had directed lots of commercials at KING-TV but had never written one. But why let a little thing like that hinder me? So I started writing commercials. The problem was, they never pleased my boss. He was kind in his criticisms, but my scripts just didn't hit the mark in his opinion.

And it wasn't just the scripts. The lighting on the ketchup wasn't bright enough; the lettuce was a little wilted; the sign wasn't straight; the music was too loud; the meat was too red; and so on and so forth. I suppose most of you have had someone in your life you couldn't please, so you know how hard it is to keep on keeping on. I would go home in tears at times, defeated and discouraged, and I wanted to leave. But the Lord seemed to be saying in my spirit, "Stay there. I have a plan for you." Since I had no peace about looking for another job, I stayed and tried to survive.

I look back at that as a wonderful learning experience in so many ways. Following God's direction caused me to do strange things like leave a promising future with the TV station and *not* leave a stressful working atmosphere at the agency. I'm sure you face difficult decisions in your career, home life, and relationships, too. I found that the more time I spent in the Bible learning about God's character and the fact that He has a perfect plan for my life, regardless of whether it made sense to me or anyone else, the more relaxed I could be while living through the circumstances surrounding the decision.

I continued at the agency, even though I wasn't getting the affirmation I needed. Then one Sunday morning, I got a call from the owner's wife asking me to come by the house. I did, and she told me the owner had died. I found a half-written commercial in his typewriter . . . so I finished it and wrote commercials for that account for the next 18 years. Not long after the owner died, I purchased the agency from his wife, and I was in business for myself.

I worked hard serving the large supermarket account, and the people there seemingly enjoyed what I was doing for them. The account grew, and they spent more money on advertising, which brought in more sales, which resulted in more money to spend on advertising. Everything they touched turned to gold. They were a force nationally in the supermarket business, and they had a lion's share of the business in almost every market they were in.

Then the supermarket had a management change. I had survived a number of such changes during my years with the account. I guess the people felt I was a part of their success and we were good teammates. But the new young manager had lots of different ideas. During the transition period with the retiring manager, the new manager told everyone at a mass meeting that there would be no changes. After all, when you're a national force, have a lion's share of the business in almost all your markets, and your sales and profits are wonderful, why fix something that isn't broken? At least that was the message we got at that first meeting.

It didn't work out that way, however. He made a number of major changes the first few months. Then he decided to put his advertising account up for review. That meant bringing in other agencies to see if he liked what they proposed better than what I was doing for him. What a slap in the face! But I knew God had a plan, and I gave the advertising manager a list of the honest agencies I would recommend he talk with. It was obvious I was on the way out, and I wanted to help them as much as I could to make a smooth transition. I saw the end coming a year or so before the new general manager actually pulled the plug, but I thought maybe I could please him, so I kept trying. I never did, though, and sometimes I'd go home from a meeting in tears because of all the stress I was feeling.

Through the years I would talk to the Lord and would ask Him, "Lord, is this really what You want me to do for the rest of my life, make money? Don't You think I should be doing more eternal things like writing books, giving seminars, and playing with my grandchildren? Why should I stay here and be miserable just to make money?"

Then a voice I'm sure only I could hear would say, "Because it pays for your ministries." Oh. So I would go back to work and do the best I could in an impossible situation.

Once again, as things went from bad to worse with the new manager, I thought about leaving, but I decided to try another tack. A few months later, I prayed, "Lord, would You cause Barb to be open about resigning from this account and doing something else?" Previously when I would take her out to talk about my miseries at work, she would tend to give me Bible verses. "Well, Isaiah 4:7 is clear on that. Romans 2 also speaks to this, and First John 4 is especially important to consider." I had no

His Other Love . . . Work   **101**

idea my problems were that simple, so I would leave our time together even more confused than ever. I wondered whether God was really paying attention to what was happening in my life. What I really needed was for someone to say it was all right to feel this way.

As I remember, my prayer was around 11:00 A.M. At noon Barb called and asked if I was "all right." She seldom called when I was with a client, but she said she just felt I was under some special strain and wanted to see if there was anything she could pray for. I told her I *was* under some special pressures and would like to go to dinner with her that night and talk about them.

At dinner, she was wonderful. She didn't give me *a single* Bible verse or easy solution. She just listened and spoke a strange language she didn't even know. She said, "What else do you feel? . . . Tell me more about that . . . What do you think we should do? . . . That's interesting. Then what did God tell you to do?"

Amazing! What a gift to give a drowning man! I wanted to resign, but neither of us had peace about doing so. We wanted the Lord to make the decision, not us. I went back to the supermarket offices the next day—and the advertising manager handed me a slip of paper confirming that the general manager wanted to look for a new agency.

So here's another principle for your life. If I had gone into the advertising office and quit as I felt like doing sometimes, that would have been *my* timing. It may or may not have been God's timing. But when the person in *authority* asks me to leave, I have to assume that God knows all about it and has approved the change.

During all my ups and downs of work, Barb was there to support me. Everywhere we lived, she created a safe haven to come home to. She never complained when money was short. She had a marvelous way of making do. I remember army housing. We couldn't afford furniture, and we needed a couch of some kind so we could have company. I went to the army surplus store and bought an old cot and a couple of mattresses.

Barb covered the mattresses with colored sheets that matched our drapes, which were also sheets, and presto, we had a couch. We put two more cots together for our bed. We bought old whiskey barrels for end tables and dressers for $1.50 at the thrift store. I really haven't thought about this in some time, and my eyes are filling with tears as I reflect that not once did she complain. She always had a sweet attitude.

We lived out of envelopes in those days. When we got our paycheck, we divided the money into envelopes for food, clothing, entertainment, car expenses, and the like. When the food envelope was empty, we didn't go shopping. We ate soup out of the cupboard until we got paid again. It is amazing to me as I think back on those days that there wasn't one time Barb didn't seem perfectly content with what she had.

We moved to Seattle after leaving the army and rented a couple of homes before finally buying one. Each one was decorated with charm and grace, and Barb kept costs within our limited means.

My career at the TV station looked good, and I'm sure Barb was secure in the knowledge that I would be a broadcaster the rest of my life. One day I told her I felt God wanted me to go on my own. She had every reason for her world to be shaky, but all I remember is her full support.

I worked out of our home for a while after leaving the TV station. Then I moved a few blocks away into an office, and since the kids were in high school, Barb and I worked together for a few years. She did all the accounting and taxes, and she managed the office. Then, our daughter Beverly came home from college and took Barb's place. Barb retired.

When it comes to my work, Barb has always been my main support and I will be eternally grateful to her for that. I realize now, however, that I was not meeting many of her relationship needs. I was always working especially when our office was at home. It was (and is) so easy to slip downstairs and just "get a few things done." By the time I got back upstairs she and the kids had gone to bed. I have really failed her often in putting my work or ministry first, and I have asked and received her forgiveness.

Getting the Right Order

Because we men get most of our self-esteem from our work, it's easy for us to lose sight of our priorities. Here's what I believe the Bible teaches as God's priorities for a husband:

1. His relationship with Jesus Christ
2. His wife
3. His children and grandchildren
4. Making a living
5. Ministry

An improper priority order may be one of the most commonly violated principles of Scripture, especially by pastors and full-time Christian workers. I've counseled a number of children of ministers who are so bitter against God because their fathers spent every waking moment at the church or ministry and never had time for them. One time Barb and I were at a conference for a national ministry. I was having lunch with the national director to talk about the agenda. When I talk with men, I always like to get the conversation around to marriage. So I asked him in effect, "How's the old marriage?" He said something like "Great!" We went back to lunch and the agenda.

Meanwhile, Barb was having lunch with his wife, and she was weeping as she told about her husband having no time for her or the family. For him, everything was ministry.

At another national ministry conference I was seated at dinner next to a man who told about his extensive travels to support his ministry. As he was talking, he was called from the table to the phone. He came back to tell us he had just prayed with his teenage son who was having a crisis at home. I just about vomited. What was he doing with an extensive ministry of traveling when his family was out of order at home? He needed to work for UPS until the kids were out of the nest, and then he could take his wife and go minister and travel.

I heard about an army chaplain who had just come home from a couple of years in an area where the family couldn't go. His ministry there was going so well that he was asked to spend another year of service in that location. His family begged him to come home, but instead, he decided to extend his service. That tears my heart out!

A man's first priority is his relationship with Jesus Christ. He can develop this on his own, but there's great value in becoming a member of some kind of accountability group such as a small-group Bible study. Accountability is greatly needed in a man's life if he is to grow spiritually. Men don't naturally reach out to anyone. We can do things "our own selves." It is hard for us to share our deepest feelings. Most of us are not into deep doctrinal thinking and discussions. We need something practical that will help us get through the day. Most of us are also not into "groups." And if we get trapped in some kind of men's retreat, many of us will probably not participate in the discussion. It is just not our nature to do so.

I suppose by now the thought might have occurred to you that the way a woman operates is exactly opposite to what I've been describing. Most women naturally reach out to make a connection with other people. Sharing feelings is a "need," not just a want. You love to delve into deep truths. You probably love retreats and women's getaways.

In my more than 60 plus years, I can't remember any men's ministries that I would call effective. Yes, there were several churches that had a Saturday morning get-together, and I'll offend some of my friends with this statement, but Saturday morning is the worst day to have such a gathering. It is the only day we men have to sleep in, take our time getting the day started, dink around the yard or garage, or attack the wife's to-do list. In my opinion, it's just not easy to have a meaningful men's ministry on Saturday morning.

But now a number of parachurch men's groups are finally taking hold, including the exploding Promise Keepers ministry.

Imagine 55,000 men in a football stadium sitting for a day and a half because they want to have better relationships with Jesus Christ and their families. That's "Red Sea" stuff. It is through his involvement with a third party—an individual or an organization—that a man becomes a disciple of Jesus Christ, and you are the beneficiary.

A man's second priority is his wife, according to Ephesians 5. He is to "die" for her as Christ died for the church. That means he gives up his life. He dies to self. He becomes her servant the way Christ became the servant of the church. Remember, He even washed the feet of His disciples.

This is extremely hard for a man. He has no idea that giving up his life means he won't be able to go hunting on Saturday because of a wedding his wife needs to go to. He doesn't understand that he has to set aside his briefcase or project to go with his wife on a date so that he can listen to her heart or discuss a conflict they are having.

What he desperately needs when he gives up his life for you is for you to tell him in words how much you appreciate his sacrifice. On the way to the wedding or anniversary or church social, tell him you realize how much of himself he is giving up. Tell him even if you don't understand how the Super Bowl or Final Four could be as important as your relationship.

Here's an assignment for one week. Sit down and make a list of all the things your husband does right. If the only thing you have on your list is that he "breathes regularly," it's okay. Then, every week notice a couple of other things and jot them down. This list is not for him, it's for YOU. Then, review the list and remind yourself to express your appreciation one more time for something good he's done. He *never* gets tired of hearing how pleased you are. Try it, and let me know how it works.

A man's third priority, according to my reading of the Scriptures, is his children and grandchildren. The hardest thing a man has to deal with regarding his children is the disagreements he and his wife have about how to raise them. She thinks he is either too soft or too hard on them. This is one of the most misunderstood conflict areas of marriage. If a husband and a wife do not agree on how to raise the children, it will take only five or six disagreements before he will silently slip back to work and delegate all child care to you.

I could write four books from the things I've learned from Dr. Dobson, Bruce Narramore, and others, but just let me say that the most critical thing a couple can do is to never disagree in front of the children about discipline, allowance amounts, or curfew times. If you do disagree, call a time-out, go into another room and resolve the disagreement. Keep the players (the children) away from the discussion while you come to a unified decision. Then announce to them that both referees have come to a decision on what the penalty or ruling will be. You can be right this time, and let your husband be right the next time. If the children sense you are not in total agreement on the final decision, they will play one of you against the other, and everyone will lose.

A fourth priority is making a living for his family. If he doesn't do this, the Bible says he is worse than an infidel. Making a living comes before teaching Sunday school, being an elder, or working with young people.

Because his work is exciting, some men will make work a number two priority, others even make it number one. Some men do this on purpose, but there are times when a man is trapped into working long hours and has no choice in the matter. Maybe he's starting a new business, working for a company that's temporarily shorthanded, or forced to work the night shift if he wants to keep his job.

We went through this tension when I was directing the evening news at the TV station. Barb explained to the kids that I would be home in time to see them if I could. I was just trapped into working evenings for the present, and the family adjusted and hoped that someday the situation would change. At least they knew they were more important than my work.

When one of my women friends read the previous sentence, she said, "How did they know?" Well, the obvious answer is that

Barb explained it to them. And then it hit me. *I* should have been the one to explain my situation to them and make sure they knew I would rather be with them than at work.

Because we men are not as sensitive as most of you women, we are going to fail at communicating that you are more important than our work. That's why God gave you to us: to complete us in all areas of life, including helping us to be sensitive and to understand how to deal with relationships.

When I had my own business I gave my employees a check and said "Thanks for doing a good job." I thought it was enough. From my standpoint I wouldn't have given them a check if they had not been doing a good job. But Barb came along and said they would like to hear the words as well as receive a check.

I know when I was running our business and someone called in sick, my inside feeling was, *What is this sick business? Can't they get on a pill program or something? I pay them to work at this desk. They should just come in and put a handkerchief over their noses, or vomit at the coffee break. I don't pay them to be sick. I pay them for work!* I hope I didn't actually send this message to my employees, but that's the way I felt. Barb didn't think such thoughts. She came right behind me with soup, suggesting they stay away from work for a couple of days to make sure they were feeling well before coming back.

Part of this attitude on my part is probably my one-dimensional focus on getting things done. What I do is what I am. I know some people will say, "You should get your self-worth from Jesus Christ, not your work." Yes, Jesus Christ should be and is the foundation for how I feel about myself, but there is also a part of me that *must* accomplish something meaningful, or I feel like a zero. This is a God-given characteristic and it's all right for me to feel this way.

It seems easier for most women to put relationships ahead of projects and accomplishments. But we men are not the same. Men in the Bible were warriors, conquerors, competitors, and builders of great cities. This is not some failure or spiritual weakness. This is the way God has designed us. Most men are restless and uneasy unless we are facing a challenge.

I had to interpret an article Barb was reading about Jimmy Johnson, a former head coach of the Dallas Cowboys football team. He was highly successful and was the only person to both play on and coach collegiate national championship football teams and win a National Football League title. In addition, he had just won back-to-back Super Bowl championships. He had a ten-year contract, and everything looked wonderful. But in the interview he said, "At times I get antsy. At times I get bored. I need a challenge." I think he reflected the attitude of most men. We can accomplish everything in sight and still not be content or satisfied without a challenge.

A short time ago, I didn't mean to, but I really hurt Barb. I was explaining to her that I felt like I had no purpose in life. She cried. Wasn't she purpose enough? Weren't all my ministries having an impact? Weren't they satisfying? Wait a minute! That's not what I was saying. Barb's not even a part of what I'm thinking about, and even if I reached the whole world with my books and seminars, I still feel I have no purpose for one reason. I am not making a living at this time. (We are living off our IRAs while we wait for our house to sell.) I think I am a rather typical male, and if I feel I have no purpose because I'm not drawing a salary, lots of other men feel the same way when they're not earning a living.

From my reading of the Bible, a man's fifth priority is ministry. My paraphrase of 1 Timothy 3:4-5 is that a man shouldn't even be asked to sweep out the church until his family is in good order. This does not mean perfect. It just means that through his servant-leadership he is meeting their needs and they are reflecting back to him this care. Now he can teach Sunday school, be an elder or pastor, work with young people, join the Awana staff, volunteer with Young Life, or be chairman of the church.

It sounds much more spiritual to preach sermons, work in the church, or counsel someone who is planning to commit suicide or file for divorce than it does to go fishing with a son or take a daughter to dinner. For a lay person, ministry comes after every-thing else. A professional clergyman can mix the priorities of work and ministry.

Please Understand About His Work

I realize that at times your husband's work seems as much of a threat as another woman. Please keep in mind that your husband's mental health depends on his feeling good about his work. I realize that sometimes he enjoys it so much that he will bring a briefcase full of work home or spend Saturdays at the office. He has no idea that he is putting you and the children behind his first love—work.

Just remember that if your husband's job is not going well, he's not going well. Or if he is out of work, he feels like a double zero. He wants to just run away somewhere. Your tender, loving patience at this time is crucial to bringing him back to life. Your approval of him can help him raise his head again and start looking for another job. You really are the only one who can give him the acceptance and unconditional love he needs as he deals with this supreme crisis in his life.

I know this is hard to do when your own security is at stake and your life is so busy and filled to the brim that you can hardly breathe. But you're the key to the future. Everyone else has rejected him. He doesn't want to be around his friends for fear they will ask him, "How's the old job hunt going?" It's not going good, and he doesn't want to have to explain. You are his only refuge in the storm. And I really believe God will give you the grace and strength to do this if you ask.

Well, we've talked quite a bit about God-designed male and female differences in how we view marriage, sex, the home, the details of life, and our approach to work. Now let's see what role personality plays in the marriage relationship.

9

Road Signs YELL at Me

Personality is not a gender trait; it's just the way we act out life's situations according to the way God has designed us. Most of the books I've read on the subject describe four basic personality types, and they all use different names. Some of the words used to describe my personality style are *driver* and *choleric*. Then there are the learning styles as described by Cynthia Tobias in a book called *The Way They Learn* .[1]

Cynthia emphasizes that we are all different and it's all right. No one style is the "right" way to do things. There is, however, one learning style, that drives all the others batty. It's called "Concrete Random," and that's me! Here are some of the characteristics she lists for my style:

Is investigative, intuitive, curious, realistic, creative, innov-
ative, divergent and adventurous.

Sees many opinions and solutions.

Contributes unusual and diverse ideas.

Lives in the future.

Hates restrictions and limitations, formal reports, routine,
re-doing anything once it's done, keeping detailed
records, showing someone how he got a particular
answer, having to choose just one answer, or having to
have no opinion on something.

Loses patience with those who can't keep up.

Jumps to conclusions without sufficient information.

Refuses to deal with problems at the time they are
brought up.

Abandons a project before it is completed.

Learns best through practical, hands-on experiences, by
inspiration, through problem solving, experiments,
open-ended activities, games and simulations, independent study, and by creating products.

Is heard to say "Why?" "I've got a really great idea," "Well
yeah, that's what I meant."

And here's the kicker.

Dislikes authority and being told what to do.

To illustrate, let me tell you a story. Barb and I were traveling to do a marriage seminar in a town on Highway 2 going to
eastern Washington. For years a sign has been on that road:
"Turn On Your Headlights. Test Area." I told Barb, "I hate that
sign!" She asked why I felt that way. "Because it's *yelling* at me,"
I answered. She thought the sign said very politely, "Pretty
please with sugar on it, would you turn on your headlights if it
isn't too much trouble?" But I heard the sign yelling, *"Turn on
your headlights (fathead)! This is a test area (stupo)!"*
The words in parentheses aren't on the sign, but that's the

way I feel every time I read it. I *never* turn on my lights. Why should I? I don't know who's giving the test. I don't know why it's taking so long to finish it. No one has ever asked me to take the test. I don't know what they're testing anyway. So why *would* I turn on my lights? Only robots would do that. And besides, I *hate* being told what to do.

When we got to the retreat, I used this little story in the seminar as I was explaining about personality styles. A guy stood up and said, "The reason for the sign is that we have lots of head-on accidents on that stretch of highway."

Okay! Now it makes sense, but for my learning style/personality, here is what the sign should read: "PLEASE turn on your headlights to prevent head-on accidents." I'd snap those lights on instantly. That sign would be meaningful. It would have value, and I would be happy to participate.

I hate it when I call the telephone directory assistance service, and after the recorded operator gives me the number, she says, "Please make a note of it (lamebrain)." Lady, I wouldn't have *called* if I hadn't planned to make a note of it so I could remember it. You don't have to tell me every time to make a note of it. I'm not stupid. Maybe I would like to *memorize* the number instead of making a note of it. You can't run my life. This is a free country! *You can't tell me what to do with a phone number.*

Excuse me, I got a little carried away there, but the operator does irritate me a great deal.

It also bothers me to get bills where the amount I owe is typed in by the computer, but there's also a little box below that says "Indicate amount paid." First of all, with light bills, insurance bills, gas bills, water bills, and mortgage bills, you either pay the entire amount or are strung up by your thumbs. The only bills I can think of where you might make a partial payment would be from department stores or credit card companies. But they *want* you to make partial payments. So, since I have to pay most bills in full, it's *dumb* to ask me how much I paid. It's right there in front of their eyes, written by their computer. So I just circle the amount with an arrow to the box.

I shouldn't even take the time to do that for such a dumb request. Maybe I'll stop it and see if they foreclose on my home.

The book *Please Understand Me* [2] provides a wonderful look at a variety of personalities. It's one of those books you can read over and over and still find something new. My son, Tim, my firstborn grandchild, Kjersten, my dog, Molly, and I have the personality called the "Apollonian" temperament. The authors, David Keirsey and Marilyn Bates, say about this style that the goal of the Apollonians is to have a goal. Their purpose in life is to have a purpose in life. No matter how they structure their relationships or time, it *must* make sense and have meaning. They are apt to be passionate in the pursuit of a creative effort; they are likely to be intellectual butterflies, who flit from idea to idea. They are future oriented and focused on what *might* be. The authors say, "In Greek mythology, Apollo stood in direct link between gods and men. They are often a self-appointed bearer of Truth, a spokesperson for the gods."

I smile when I read that description because that is *exactly* Barb's perception of me. Early on, one of her favorite comments was, "When the king speaks, no one speaks after the king." I didn't mean to come off kingly—I just happen to be *right* in most situations. That's not my fault. That's the way God made me—His design; His plan; His goal; His desire; His passion. (Are you convinced yet?) He wants me to be His representative to you mortals here on earth. It's a high calling, and I'm happy to do it.

Dr. Grant Martin wrote a book called *The Hyperactive Child*, based in part on the work of R. A. Barkley in his book *Attention-Deficit Hyperactivity Disorder* (ADHD). Although I have never been diagnosed as someone with ADHD, I have a lot of the characteristics of one. In his work, Dr. Martin indicated that the social scientists have not determined whether ADHD continues into adulthood. Well, here's good news, Dr. Martin: The scientists don't have to spend one more dollar in research. If they'll just interview me or ask Barb, they'll have all the proof they need that it does, indeed. I'm just a layperson, so

I'll be giving you my unofficial opinions on all this, but please check me out by reading the experts I've listed in the resources at the end of the book.

I can fully relate to Martin's and Barkley's descriptions of what the ADHD child would do with a pencil:

Blow it across the desk.
Fly it through the air.
Hold it high in the air and drop it.
Stick it in the screws of the chair.
Thread it through his belt loops.
Pick the threads of his socks.
Roll it inside his desk.
Poke his neighbor.
Sharpen and re-sharpen it.
Lose it.

Not only can I relate, but I also thought of a few more on my own:

Balance it on the tip of his nose.
See if he can balance it on one finger straight up with the
    point down.
Store it behind his ear.
Store it behind his *neighbor's* ear.
Stick it *in* his ear for a while.
Hold it under his nose with your upper lip.
Stick it in his hair.
Balance it on his desk.
Balance it on another pencil.
Flip spit wads with it like a catapult.

In my opinion, the experts' description of ADHD fits almost exactly the Concrete Random (CR) learning style detailed by Cynthia Tobias. The tragedy of all this is that some people are *drugging* kids (primarily with Ritalin) to bring them into conformity with what's "normal" and they may not have the disorder at all. Let me quickly add that I personally know children who simply would not survive without chemical help. All I'm saying is that many kids are being misdiagnosed simply because they seem to be out of step with everyone else.

Here are some of the characteristics of an ADHD person that fit me as a person with the CR style: *trouble directing and sustaining attention in conversations, lectures, reading, instructions, and driving.* To me, a conversation *must* be meaningful in some way. Someone needs to be on the verge of a divorce, suicide, business failure, parenting problem, depression, or financial struggle in order for me to sustain an interest for long. It's extremely hard for me to stay with a conversation on subjects I find meaningless, like ball scores, the weather, or someone's vacation plans.

Lectures bore me to death. I hate to shock you, but many *sermons* also bore me to death. Who wants to be preached at or lectured to with no chance to interact or debate the pros and cons of a subject?

As for having trouble maintaining a sustained interest in reading, I have probably 2,000 books staring down at me from the shelves in the study where I'm writing these words. I have another couple hundred on shelves in other rooms of the house. I probably have 50 by and under my side of the bed. Okay, there *is* one negative to this, and that is that our insurance policy doesn't cover us when we make the bed. If we trip over one of the 50 books I have by the bed, we have to pay the hospital bills. The insurance company told me it is simply not going to take that sort of risk.

I read when I go to bed, but there's no reason to keep reading the same book. Sometimes I'll change books two or three times a night. I might start with a Calvin and Hobbes cartoon book for a good laugh. Then I'll switch to a book where I can learn something, and I underline the main points. That keeps me interested and awake. When I want to go to sleep, I switch to a political or history book, and I'm snoring before I've turned a couple of pages.

I *have* finished quite a few books, but I've started hundreds more that I probably will never finish. No, I'm not good at sustaining reading if you mean starting a book and then finishing it before starting another.

Yes, I also have problems sustaining an abiding interest in instructions. I *hate* to read instructions. I read them only when I get stuck. I was putting together a metal building at our cabin one time. What's it take to put a metal building together? You have four walls, a roof, a couple of doors—no big deal. Why in the world would you bother with instructions? So I assembled it.

When I stepped back to admire my work, I stumbled over a bag of white things. So I checked the instructions under "white things" and found out they were the 500 grommets I should have put under the roof screws to keep the roof from leaking. This might not be a problem where you live, but here in Seattle it's a major concern. Being a true creative ADHD (CR), I just took my caulking gun and zapped all the screws, and not one drop of rain has ever seeped through the roof. It doesn't *look* as professional as if Barb had put the shed up, but we don't take our visitors out there anyway, so who cares? And I haven't spent the sunset years of my life reading instructions.

Another trait of an ADHD person that fits me is *difficulty completing projects; a lack of stick-to-itiveness.* I've yet to find a Bible verse that says I have to finish everything I start. I've heard a lot of structured *people* say that, but I can't seem to find it in Scripture. I haven't found one person who can give me a good reason why I need to do something for more than 10 or 15 minutes at a time, with the exception of the things Barb needs. But for everyone else, it doesn't matter. The fun part is *starting* projects, not finishing them.

A third characteristic of an ADHD is *easily overwhelmed by the task of daily living.* And just this *week*, I've been looking over the edge. I say yes to way too many things. I'm challenged by having a number of things going at once. I'm like the guy at the circus with 100 plates spinning on sticks. He goes around respinning the ones that wobble just before they fall. I like that because it feeds my creative juices. But when 10 of them wobble at the same time, then I'm overwhelmed. I'm not sure that's a chemical deficiency as much as a wimpy backbone that can't say no.

I also get overwhelmed with what I would consider complicated projects that have to be analyzed and studied. For instance, I have the software for several financial packages that would help me keep track of our money and investments. In fact, I've had one for about eight years. I just can't seem to find the time to study the directions. The instruction book is six inches thick and starts out:

> Dear Customer,
> Thank you for buying our product. Using the transient megahertz flim-flam, recogitate the egnoiter switch making sure that the blotzfinder is firmly established in the grindenshafter. Of course, having already zipozed the chunkits, now taeoisze the kersnosendripper, etc., etc.

I close the book each time and decide I'll learn to install the software later.

Yet another ADHD trait is *trouble maintaining an organized living/work place*. For the life of me, I can't find anyone who can give me a good reason (other than a mate's needs) why we have to have an organized work or living place. I have piles of things all over the house—that is, until you come to visit. Then I'll cram the stuff under the bed, in the closet, or in my rolltop desk, and you'll think I'm a neatnik. I do that for Barb and Barb alone. She's the only one who cares. Yet to my amazement, I know of structured people in our world who think being unorganized is something so bad or undesirable that drugs are the only answer to help the person in question "shape up."

Inconsistent work performance is also an ADHD tendency. I'm not sure what that means, but it sounds as if some days you feel like working 10 hours, and some days you want to take a nap in the afternoon. It sounds, too, as if some people work best from

8:00 P.M. to 3:00 A.M., while people like me see their brains turn
to jelly around 6:00 P.M., yet we're bright, alert, and creative at
6:30 A.M. if we can convince ourselves it's important to get up.
This "deficiency" sounds like a person who does not conform to
someone else's criteria rather than someone who has a character flaw.

Lacks attention to detail, the ADHD manuals further state.
Check *Strong's Bible Concordance* to see if you can come up with
a Bible verse that says not being into details is a horrible thing
or a sin. Maybe you can find one. I surely can't. This sounds to
me like a structured bean counter's rule.

I'm a big-picture, visionary type of person. I'll have 19 ideas
on the way to work, 18 of which would be instant successes, but
I have no one to do all the detail work. It's not my gift to go to
the courthouse and wade through cobwebs looking for a zoning
ordinance, get a license, look for a rental, negotiate a selling
price, or see if there's enough parking or curb space. What I
want to do is give my idea to others and have *them* do the detail
work. I'll then come up with 19 more world-changing ideas.
Details are not my thing, and there's no reason on earth why I
should try to change that.

I can't even find my way to my brother-in-law's house unless
Barb is with me, and I've been there at least 200 times. Barb
and I always go together when we visit him. I don't have to
notice street signs or landmarks. I just drive as Barb directs until
she says stop, and then I get out.

ADHD people *also make decisions impulsively and don't antic-
ipate consequences.* Guilty as charged, but *I'm* the one who
suffers from my impulsive decisions, so no one else should be
concerned—except, that is, for Barb. And I made a commitment to her that I would never make a unilateral decision if it
involved her, family money, or priorities, so she's protected from
my impulsiveness.

A person with ADHD also *has difficulty delaying gratification;
seeks out stimulation.* Why do you think I'm 20 pounds overweight?

Is restless and fidgety, they also say. Especially during lectures and sermons.

Makes statements without considering their impact, the experts advise. Reread the last few pages. If I carefully considered the impact of my statements, I probably wouldn't have been so candid and honest. But I hope my directness will be helpful to you as you try to understand other people and save some precious kids from the structured folks who want them to be "normal."

Impatient the books say. I've always had a problem with impatience and I doubt I need to tell you about that. On the other hand, sometimes I'm *too* patient with people, especially salespersons. At the state fair, I'm an easy mark for those fast talkers under umbrellas who sell salad makers, kazoos, tattoos, blown glass, and knives that will never dull.

Not long after we were first married, Barb and I went to the fair. We stopped to see a man demonstrating a blender. We were amazed. It chewed up ice, rocks, whole potatoes, and a screwdriver. The guy threw in a hammer: *poof*, it vaporized. There was nothing the blender wouldn't chew up as it combined lots of good things to make delicious drinks for our health's sake. We decided we would be the laughing stock of the neighborhood if we didn't have a blender, so we purchased one.

Thinking back, I'm sure the man was honest, because at no time did he actually say *our* blender would do the same things *his* blender did. He was simply demonstrating what a blender could do if you had a 10-horsepower table-saw motor under the table. He just *happened* to have a stack of blenders on the table that resembled his, just in case anyone wanted to buy a blender that *looked* like his. He was perfectly innocent of any wrongdoing, I'm sure.

On the way home, I had visions of growing as strong as Charles Atlas (the Arnold Schwarzenegger of my day) with all the nutritious drinks our new blender would be churning out. In fact, I wanted to stop at a men's store to get a new wardrobe for my bulging new muscles, but Barb thought we should get home.

I unpacked the new blender and excitedly put in some water, the screwdriver, some ice, my watch, and the artichoke hearts that were going to make me strong. Then I pushed the button. Our blender groaned a little and blew a fuse. So I took out the screwdriver and watch and tried again. Another fuse blew. So I took everything out except the water, and it took right off. But in a couple of seconds, the motor began to smoke from the drag of the water. We have heavy water in Washington state, so I shouldn't have been surprised. We still have that blender somewhere. After I spent so much money on it, there was no way I was going to get rid of it.

Another characteristic of an ADHD (CR) person is *being easily frustrated*. That fits me, too. I'm very frustrated when I run out of staples or when someone doesn't hang up my tools, loses the scissors, is standing in *my* bank line, is in front of me at *my* favorite restaurant and I'm starving to death, or starts reconstructing *my* freeway without first checking with me. You bet those things make me frustrated, and sometimes (hold on to your socks) they make me *angry*, if you can believe that.

My purpose here is not to criticize the doctors who give out Prozac and Ritalin. All I want you to know is that my CR learning style fits the characteristics of the ADHD person almost 100 percent. We just need to remember that what may look like ADHD may only be a CR learning style.

Having a CR learning style is not a sin, and I haven't hurt anyone except Barb, whose forgiveness I've asked and received for those times when I've messed up her life. In all the other areas of my life, my CR nature has been harmless. I have a stamp collection with all the plate blocks and individual stamps I've saved since high school. That sounds like a strange hobby for a changeable person like me who is not into details and not very structured, but I'll show it to you sometime when you drop by. I have all the stamp albums I need to put them in, too. I have all the stamps in boxes, and someday I'll get around to putting them *into* the books. I've been extra busy ever since high school and just haven't gotten to it. But don't worry. I will.

One of these days.

I also collect coins, another strange activity for a CR impulsive person. I collect them in cans. Don't rush me. Someday I'll get them into the coin books.

I *have* bothered Barb a little with my goal-oriented nature. Years ago I used to give her a list of goals to accomplish. She would get one or two done and then want to enjoy her success. But because of my personality style, I would point to the next item on the list and ask her, "When are you going to get *this* done?" Therefore, she didn't think I appreciated the ones she *had* achieved. Remember, my chief goal in life is to have a goal. So what's the logical thing to do when you've accomplished a goal? Set another, of course. But Barb wants to *rest,* if you can believe that. She seems to enjoy the *process* of getting something done more than I do.

When I want to present a new goal to Barb, I will say, "I've been thinking." That scares her, because those are the same words I used when we were talking about our wedding. "I've been thinking we could get married after my two years in the army." A few days later: "I've been thinking we could get married at the end of the summer." A few days later: "I've been thinking we could get married at the *start* of the summer, after school is over." A few days later: "I've been thinking we could get married between semesters of my senior year."

"Enough with the thinking!" said her mom. So we were married between semesters.

I guess there is one tiny, teeny, minute problem we impulsive, goal-oriented people get into once in a while. Many of our great ideas involve money, and we have a need to accomplish the idea *right now.* Barb says that's okay if you can afford it, but so often we can't.

I didn't know this, but for nine years Barb had waited to buy new carpet for the first home we owned. This was when I was starting my own production company for radio and TV commercials. She was keeping the financial books for the company, and she would see where we were going to have enough money to buy the carpet—until I told her at the exact same time that I needed another piece of business equipment. Since I used the equipment to provide for the family, when Barb would ask me about the purchase, I would say, "But it's for *you.*" For some reason, however, she didn't *feel* as if it were for her. But didn't she understand she wouldn't eat unless I got paid for commercials, and I couldn't do commercials if I didn't have the right equipment, so I never quite understood why she resisted the thought that the equipment was for her.

Barb says that when I tell her about a goal, I make it sound as if it's the most important thing in the world to me. In fact, it is—at that moment. Barb thinks about it, decides to go along with my idea, and begins to adjust to my way of thinking. She says I've sold her on the idea with all the conviction in the world. She feels I would even sign a contract in blood if she asked me to. So she begins following along, but in a few weeks I've decided to do something else. It drives her crazy.

Another goal of mine is to figure out how to do things the easy way, and that, too, bothers her. Sometimes I would have a wheat germ, peanut butter, and honey combination for break-fast. Then Barb would complain because there were drips of honey coming down the side of the jar after I put it away, which made the cupboard shelf sticky. So I got a plastic dish and put the honey in it upside down so I wouldn't have to wait for the honey to run out of the jar. Now the cupboard stays unsticky, and I get on with my life.

Then there are those times when Barb goes to visit her family in Wenatchee and leaves me to tend the house myself. Why should I make the bed when I'm just going to get back in it tonight, get out of it tomorrow morning, and get back in it again tomorrow night? It seems like such a waste of energy to keep making it all the time. And then there's the dishes. We have dishes in the cupboard that we haven't used since our wedding 40 years ago. We keep washing the ones in the front row, so we never get to the back. We take a few out, use them, wash them, and put them back over and over. We have some of

Edison's first dishes that have never seen the light of day.

When Barb is gone, I use new dishes from the cupboard each day and put them in the sink after I eat. They stack neatly. The plates fit nicely with other plates, the saucers with other saucers, and the cups with other cups. It looks very orderly. And they say a CR person can't be orderly! Then, just before Barb comes *home*, I make the bed and wash the dishes *once*. Everyone's happy.

I've talked a lot about the mistakes I have made, but I don't want you to think Barb is absolutely perfect. Take her pantry, for instance. You have to be very careful, because the potatoes have long sprouts on them that reach out and trip you deliberately when you go by. Once in a while I go to the refrigerator and a fuzzy green feeler lashes out at me from one of the Tupperware dishes holding leftovers. That's the macaroni and cheese from Christmas.

Also I remember the time when we were bumped up to first class on one of our airline trips. We had never thought the extra money was worth the prestige, but we were excited when we found ourselves up in the linen napkin compartment. A tragedy happened, however. Barb dropped her dinner roll, and we've never been asked back since. I think it rolled all the way back to the tail of the airplane and embarrassed the flight attendants who like things orderly.

And here's the most serious flaw in Barb's character. It's the reason I could never run for president of the United States. The reporters are sure to dig this skeleton out of our closet. Barb used to be addicted to Häagen-Dazs Rum Raisin Ice Cream. She has even been known to, hang on to your bonnets, eat a whole pint at one sitting. I can see the headlines now: EXTRA! EXTRA!! PRESIDENTIAL CANDIDATE SNYDER WITHDRAWS FROM RACE DUE TO WIFE'S ADDICTION. See? She's not so perfect.

When He Marches to a Different Drum Beat

My main purpose for going into so much detail on my own personality style is to remind you that it is okay to be different.

Each partner needs to spend energy supporting and understanding the other person rather than trying to change the person into a copy of himself/herself. If we feel okay about how God designed us, we can be of benefit to others who are struggling.

I was talking with a couple after one of our seminars. I always like to bring up the subject of CRs just in case one of the people I'm talking with is one. I listed a few characteristics of the CR, and they just looked at each other in amazement. With some mystical magic I had just described not one of them, but their 14-year-old son. They had him in "chains" just like I did my son Tim when he was that age.

I explained that CR kids are always just a half step different than anyone else and always have another opinion. They agreed, and used the example of their wanting to go for fish and chips after the seminar, but their CR son wanted to go for pizza. Now from my standpoint, both as a grandfather and as a person who has learned a lot about CR children, I asked, "What was wrong with going for pizza?" I don't think it had ever occurred to the parents they could go for pizza when they wanted to go for fish and chips. I suppose it sounded to them like the son was being rebellious and resistant and wanted control. I don't know about the rebellious and resistant part but I do know the CR person must feel he has at least some control over his life. What is so wrong about going for pizza for the few short years you have the CR in your home? Nothing that I can think of except cholesterol, and you get that just by breathing.

We were vacationing at a friend's cabin recently, and I noticed a picture on the wall that made my heart sing. It was a flock of birds on the beach with all their beaks headed in one direction, except one bird right in the middle of the crowd. He was going down the beach the exact *opposite* way. I was in trouble all week with Barb looking at that picture and saying "THAT'S YOU!" I wasn't offended. Actually I was excited to be reminded that it is okay to have independent opinions and not necessarily agree with everything you see or read or hear. Jesus Christ spent most of His time bucking the trends of His day. I can hardly wait to compare CR stories with Him after He takes me home.

Help Him Become All He Can Be

Do you allow your husband to be different without giving him a bad time or wanting to change him? I hope you'll take the time to read some of the books I have suggested that explain the various personalities and learning styles. Then when you find a description of your husband, you can relax and realize that other women have experienced the same kinds of struggles you have in living with a person like him. And maybe you'll be able to get to the point of actually THANKING God for making your special completer so different as you learn how his special gifts complement yours.

One of the most common causes of marriage DISharmony, in my opinion, is that neither partner allows the other person to be who he or she IS. Each visualizes the other as "wrong" and tries to make the partner over. The sooner you can accept your mate as being exactly like God intended him to be, rather than one of His mistakes, the sooner your marriage will begin to be everything you would like it to be and you'll start to have fun again.

I was struck by the wisdom in a series of statements from the book *Please Understand Me*:

"If I do not want what you want, please try not to tell me that my want is wrong."

"Or if I believe other than you, at least pause before you correct my view."

"Or if my emotion is less than yours, or more, given the same circumstances, try not to ask me to feel more strongly or weakly."

"I do not, for the moment at least, ask you to understand me. That will come only when you are willing to give up CHANGING me into a copy of you."

"To put up with me is the first step to understanding me. Not that you embrace my ways as right for you, but that you are no longer irritated or disappointed with me for my seeming waywardness. And in understanding me you might come to PRIZE my differences from you, and, far from seeking to change me, preserve and even nurture those differences."[3]

Personality styles are not wrong, just different. Both the husband and the wife must write this principle on the doorways of their hearts to fully appreciate the gifts the marriage partner brings to the relationship. It's not easy, but it IS possible with God's help and your obedience to His principles of love, acceptance, and forgiveness.

Everyone knows that communication differences can cause marriage strife. But did you know that some of the differences are caused by brain wiring? That's coming up next.

10

I Would Have Remembered If You'd Told Me You Were Pregnant!

I think Barb is missing a gene or something, because when she communicates with me, she often asks questions without wanting answers.

For instance, when we decide to go out to eat, I want to go where she feels like eating, so I will ask her, "Where do you want to eat?"

She'll say, "I don't care. Where do *you* want to eat?"

I'll say, "I don't care. Where do *you* want to eat?"

She'll say, "I don't care. Where do *you* want to eat?"

Okay, it sounds as if she wants to know where I would like to eat, so I say, "Let's go someplace where we can get fish and chips."

Then she'll say "*YYYuuuuuuuucckkk.* What do you think about chicken?"

I could have sworn she said, "Where do *you* want to eat?"

This might be a hormone problem, but it's more likely a principle Barb and I have learned about men's and women's communication. When a man gives his opinion, a woman takes it as his opinion. That's the way he feels about something. When a woman gives her opinion, however, the man usually takes it as a *command*. He says something like, "All right, have it your way. I was only making a suggestion," and then he cuts off communication. When I say, "How about fish and chips?" and Barb says "What about chicken?" it doesn't occur to me to carry the discussion any further. As far as I'm concerned, she has made the decision, and it's up to me to go along with it.

Or we'll go to a stadium or theater where our seats are not assigned, and I'll say, "Where do you want to sit?"

She'll say, "I don't care. Where do *you* want to sit?"

It sounds as if she's saying, "Where do you want to sit?" so I'll say, "How about here?"

Then she'll say, "No, let's go down front."

Why *ask* if she doesn't want my opinion?

I'm easy. I'll eat and go sit anywhere she wants. Barb says she thinks we're still discussing it. It surely doesn't sound like a discussion to me when *she* decides where we'll eat or sit and won't take my suggestion.

Or consider the fact that Barb feels deadlines are guidelines. I think we should be on time wherever we go. It took me a while to figure out what was happening with her. I would be outside our home in the car, waiting to leave for church or somewhere, but no Barb. I would wait a while and then go back into the house to find her, and guess what she would be doing? Making the beds, cleaning the kitchen, or hanging up the kids' clothes. What in the world do those things have to do with being somewhere on time? I guess she just didn't want to come home to the mess, and that was more important to her than being on time.

I also believe God wants us to be on time for things like airport schedules. Scripture says we're to be at the airport one hour before our flight takes off. I can't put my finger on the exact verse right now, but trust me. When Barb and I are in the planning stage, she will ask me when I think we should leave for the airport. I hate to give an opinion because I know it will be wrong, but eventually, I'll say, "How about 10:30?"

She'll think a minute and then say, "How about 11:00?"

If she didn't want to take my suggestion, why did she ask? I'll never understand why she wants me to make a decision if she's going to change it.

Also, Barb thinks restaurant menus are guidelines. From my standpoint, the leaders of commerce spend millions of dollars every year planning, printing, and distributing menus. The way to order from a menu is simply to say, "I'll have number one with whole wheat toast."

Barb, however, wants to *change* number one on the menu. She'll say, "May I have two salads, please, one with blue cheese dressing and one with French, and I want my dressing on the side, and I would like my toast almost burned, but dry, and don't let the cook put any butter on the fish. Do you have any orange marmalade? I only want half a cup of coffee for now, and do you have some lemon wedges for my water?" It used to embarrass me when Barb would upset our nation's economy so badly by making the poor waiter go through all those hoops.

One time we attended an event at the convention center in downtown Seattle. I let Barb off at the door as I usually do, then went to park. After the program was over, I started for the door near where our car was parked, but for some reason Barb thought we should go another way. I had parked the car. She had no idea where it was. But I am so tuned in to going along with what Barb wants that we walked completely around the center, through dark alleys and mugging parks, before we finally got to the car. We laughed, but she wanted to know why I hadn't been firm about taking the shortest route. I didn't have a good answer for her. I just wanted to go along with her wishes, even though I knew where the car was parked.

A couple of my men friends were shocked when I shared this

story with them. I sound like such a wimp or doormat to go the wrong way to the parking lot just because my wife thought she knew which way to go. However, in my mind, I look at this as proof that I am totally committed to meeting as many of Barb's needs as I can. We were having fun. I enjoy being with her. A little extra time going around the block didn't seem like that big a deal.

By now you know I kid around a lot about life's situations, but I want you to know about a very serious difference between men and women, and that is the fact that our brains are wired differently. Dr. Donald Joy has talked about this on "Focus on the Family." I don't pretend to have all the details, but evidently, a male baby's brain is bathed with a hormone early in its development that destroys many of the interconnecting fibers between the two halves of the brain—not all the fibers, but most of them. A girl baby doesn't experience this, so she is born with numerous interconnecting fibers between the two hemispheres of her brain.

One thing this brain wiring does is make a man more one-dimensional and focused. That doesn't mean he can't use both sides of his brain. It simply means he usually is using only one side at a time. He might be figuring math problems, learning a language, or examining technical details with his left side, or painting a picture, listening to music, or writing a book with his right side. He moves back and forth, depending on what he's working on.

An example of this would be Monday night football. Let's say I'm watching the Seattle Seahawks maul the Dallas Cowboys (a little fantasy never hurt anyone). It's an important game, and I'm really into it. All of a sudden, I am vaguely aware of a disturbance in the room. It gets louder and louder, and finally, I realize Barb is trying to communicate with me. I always advise wives not to try to talk with their husbands until half-time, but here is Barb trying to get my attention to tell me that the roof blew off, the furnace exploded, one of our children is trapped in a tree, or some other insignificant household detail.

She finally gets loud enough to break through my concentration on the game. You see, I don't know I'm married or have three* kids, a furnace, a roof, or live in the United States. All I know is that if our running back doesn't make third and long, we're in big trouble. I'm completely innocent if Barb tries to talk with me and I don't hear her. At that moment, I don't even know she exists.

I've even heard of a wife making cutting remarks like, "You never hear anything I say," "You never talk to me," or "Well, if you didn't hear me, you can just forget dinner!" and she heads out the door in a huff just as the husband looks up. He didn't know she was speaking to him. He's innocent. He loves her, and if that ever changes, he'll let her know. But at the moment, he's watching a football game, and he can't communicate with her and watch the game at the same time.

Or there are those times when I'm reading a magazine. I don't even know Barb is in the house, but all of a sudden I glance up and she's looking at me and saying, "Isn't that right?" or "What do you think about that?" Again, I didn't know I had a wife. I was into my magazine.

Here's the principle, ladies. Just because your mouth is opening and closing does not mean your husband or sons are hearing you when they're concentrating on something. When Barb wants my attention, she takes my head in her hands and looks into my eyes. They will be glazed over a bit, but she doesn't panic. She just says something like, "Testing, testing, Barb to Chuck, Barb to Chuck." Then my eyes will unglaze, I'll remember that I'm married, Barb can tell me anything she wants to, and I'll hear her. One more time. Don't expect your husband to automatically hear you just because you're speaking. Make sure you have his attention before you begin. A soft blow with a two-by-four also works quite well.

On the other hand, because Barb's brain wasn't "damaged" at birth, she is multiaware of things around her. When we go to a baseball game, she takes her handwork, talks to several of the players' wives, and soon knows who's angry, who's pregnant, and who's lonely. She can tune in on three or four conversations at

---

* We adopted our daughter Debbie when she was 34 years old, so I didn't include her upbringing in the chapter on children.

once. She knows the score of the game and where Rick the peanut guy is—all at the same time. All I know is that if Randy Johnson doesn't strike out this last batter, we could lose the game.

You women think we men are equal to you mentally. But because of this brain wiring difference, we aren't. Barb often forgets to give me all the information I need to keep up with her. For instance, on the third-floor living area of our home, I have a shower in my bathroom, and Barb has a bathtub in hers. Once in a while, she'll come over to use the shower in the morning while I'm shaving. One time she was showering, and she called out, "Is the hot water on?"

"No," I said.

"Put it on, please," she said.

So I turned on the hot water in the sink. I thought maybe it was affecting the water temperature of her shower. And I kept on shaving.

She didn't understand why I didn't leave the bathroom. What I didn't know was that she had asked if I would *turn on the hot water under the coffee* down in the kitchen. She had neglected to say three essential words: under the coffee. She thought I should just *know* what she meant.

I also recall a time when we were in an airplane during a layover. We usually have aisle seats across from each other. At our age, we get up and down a lot, and that arrangement makes it easier. Barb had a seatmate on her side of the plane, so she took all her carry-on material up to a vacant seat so she could have more room to work on her Bible study. We decided to stay on the plane during the layover, and after it had cleared out, she called back, "Is my seatmate gone?"

"Yes, he's gone," I said. I had seen him leave.

So she gathered up all her books and papers and came back to her seat, but his stuff was still under the seat. She was amazed that I had said he was gone when obviously he wasn't. I was supposed to catch the difference between "Is he gone?" (forever) and "Is he gone?" (until the plane takes off again). I think that's asking a lot.

Another time, we were on our way in the car to speak at a conference. We were just driving along, and Barb said, "You'll enjoy meeting her." Well, I'm sure I would, but I didn't know who "her" was nor where I would meet her. Was she a member of our Sunday school class, Barb's Bible study group, or some extended family member coming to the conference? I didn't have much to go on, yet Barb thought I should know whom she meant.

Barb and I were reading the paper at the breakfast table one day. All of a sudden, she put down her part of the paper and said, "Will you have what's-his-name fix that thing?" Can you get many clues from that statement about who should fix what? But Barb thought I should know.

We just got back from a cabin where I was trying to finish this book. On vacation, I feel free to have white bread, baloney, eggs and bacon, a nice steak, baked potatoes with more things on top than most people think is healthy, and all the pop I want to drink. I usually conform more to Barb's nutritional standards at home, but on vacation I want to eat the way I will when I get to heaven. So I did all that and was enjoying myself immensely at the dinner table when Barb said, "Who do you want to give money gifts to when you die?"

I thought she had agreed not to give me a bad time about my vacation eating. What she had forgotten to tell me, however, was that she was thinking about the owner of the cabin, who had recently lost her husband. I needed some sort of introductory statement like, "I was thinking of all the grief Annie has gone through because of her husband's death, yet she was able to give cash gifts to some of the organizations she admires." Then the question about my dying would have been a little less abrupt.

And there are those times when Barb *swears* she told me something, and I'm equally sure those words never came out of her mouth. She was talking to her mom, a girlfriend, the butcher, or the neighbor, but she never brought up the subject within *my* hearing range. I'm sure she said to the neighbor, "I think I'll ask Chuck to take out the garbage," but she never asked me. She'll tell her friends, "I think I'll have Chuck clean the gutters this weekend," but I never get the message.

Even worse, Barb sometimes just *thinks* about something and then is sure she mentioned it to me out loud. My feeling is, I'm *sure* I would have remembered something that important if she had told me. We saw a cartoon once where the wife was in the kitchen preparing dinner, the husband was reading his paper, and a baby was crawling across the floor. The husband says, "I *know* I would have remembered if you had told me you were pregnant!"

Many wives do not give proper transitions, either. We will be driving along in the car, talking about Aunt Suzie's haircut, and all of a sudden, Barb will start giving some details that have nothing to do with the subject at hand. I'll listen to a bit of it and ask what that has to do with Aunt Suzie's haircut, only to find out Barb is now talking about Uncle Ted's violin. Or she will be talking about how wonderful Dan is, so I'm going along with her in my mind that Dan Wilson is a great person, when all of a sudden, she'll mention his home in Kirkland. Dan Wilson doesn't live in Kirkland, so I challenge her and find out she's talking about Dan Washburn. He's also a great guy, but now I have to go back over the whole conversation and bring my brain up to date with the new name. She thinks it should be obvious who she's talking about.

It could be that this brain damage prevents husbands from finding things in cupboards. Barb will ask me to get something for her from the kitchen cupboard. I look for it, but it's not there, and I come back empty-handed. So Barb will urge her tired body out of the chair, go to the cupboard and move something, and there it is. I didn't know I was supposed to *move* anything. I figured it should be in the front row. I get in trouble because she doesn't give me clear directions such as: "It could be in the second row, so you might have to *move* something." I could have found it easily with those clear, concise instructions. I don't know why she can't be more accurate when she makes a request.

Sometimes when Barb asks me to find something and I can't, she can't find it, either. Instead of being in the cupboard, it was on the stove or by the sink. Rather than apologizing, she tee-hees and makes a big joke about her telling me it was somewhere it wasn't. It's World War III when I don't find something, but when *she* can't find it, either, it's the comedy hour. Sounds like a double standard to me.

It Ain't Easy

It's hard to know where to begin, because communication is so complicated. Some of the problem is the result of the man being focused on what he's doing, and since the woman is multiaware, she wonders why he isn't, too. Much of it is different personality styles. Maybe one person is subjective and reads things into what the other is saying, then comes up with the wrong answer.

I tend to be subjective. Once when I was preparing some cheese for a snack, I cut a piece and put it on a plate so I could soften it in the microwave. Barb said, "Boy, that's a big piece of cheese." Because of my extra pounds and subjective thinking, what I heard her say was, "Listen, chubby, you don't need all that cheese." She swears all she meant by her statement was that the cheese would not melt very well in the microwave. It would burn the edges before melting. I felt guilty about my weight, so I wrapped the cheese and put it back in the refrigerator and stomped angrily out of the room. Barb just stood there saying to herself, "Who was that masked man?" Everything that had caused the communication breakdown was in my mind. She had no idea of what went wrong.

I've offended Barb many times with my negative thinking, so we have found a technique called "short accounts." When I have a negative thought, I have to ask Barb about it. I say, "Barb, it seems like you are just a little uptight right now. Have I done something to bother you?" This allows us to talk about it. Often I'm not even involved. But if I don't ask the question, then I turn the negative to myself and get angry or depressed and offend Barb without her knowing why.

Or maybe one person is expressive and one is nonexpressive.

Expressive people know immediately how they feel, even in a conflict situation. Nonexpressive people don't have a *clue* as to why they're angry or upset, *especially* in a conflict situation. At least 80 percent of the couples that come into my life for counseling are struggling with this difference in their personality styles.

A wonderfully practical way to solve conflicts between expressive and nonexpressive people is with a concept called "quick listening." I first learned about this technique in a management seminar where we were to find a partner and select a controversial subject on which we disagreed. Then each of us was to express thoughts on the subject for two minutes without interruption. I saw people change sides when they heard the other position given for the first time without interruption. When was the last time you spoke to your mate for two minutes without interrupting or being interrupted?

Barb likes the two-minute rule, but I think it was made up by some expressive type like her. If I am interrupted, I lose my train of thought and finally just quit and say, "Everything's fine," when it isn't. My rule is that a nonexpressive person should have longer than two minutes so that he can finish what he has to say. The first time Barb and I did this she said, "Just keep it short!" I think and talk slow and have trouble putting my feelings into words. But by the time I get all my feelings out on the table, I'm not angry anymore. I can look down on my feelings and say, "I'm sorry. I didn't realize I did that. Please forgive me."

The process takes compromise on both sides. The expressive person has to keep a moderately happy face for a few days while the problem remains unsolved. The nonexpressive person has to give his partner hope he or she will talk about it. To someone like me, conflictive communication is a little like vomiting. I am doing something I hate, but I do feel better when it's over.

I want to give you some hope. Men can be taught how to communicate and meet your needs. I've learned. John Kasay's learned. He was a placekicker for the Seattle Seahawk football team. He did an internship with my advertising agency several years ago to complete some school requirements. We had a great time. He was very structured, as you would imagine a kicker to be. He planned and executed every project I gave him in a professional manner.

One day we were talking, and he mentioned that his wife, Laura, was having some problems in her life, but she was *not* taking his advice. He could see clearly what she should do, but she wasn't listening to him. What could he do?

I had him get his legal tablet so he could write some things down and memorize them. I suggested that the next time Laura discussed some of her problems with him, he should refer to the tablet in his mind and say strange, unnatural things (for him) like these: "I'll bet that ties you up in knots, doesn't it?" "That must be frustrating for you"; "Tell me more about that"; "What else do you feel?"; "My, my"; "Then what happened?"

He wrote them all down, and when he came in the next day, he was excited. He said he and Laura went for a walk the previous evening, and she shared a feeling with him. He then mentally looked at his tablet and said, "I'll bet that ties you up in knots, doesn't it?"

John said Laura stopped, took off *his* sunglasses so she could see his eyes, and said, *"What did you just say?"* He repeated what he had said, and she started laughing. Then she said something like, "You've been talking to *Chuck,* haven't you?" And then she started to describe some more things that had been troubling her. Half the time she laughed and *knew* what he was doing when he asked feeling questions, and half the time she really thought he wanted to hear her heart. He *did.* He just had not known how before. When he thought she was asking for advice or solutions to her problems, all she really wanted was understanding.

I was John's "third party," just like Gary Smalley was for me years ago. I know the concept might be a little frustrating for some of you because your natural question is, "Where can I find a third party for my man?" It can be as simple as buying a few of the many books and tapes on marriage and communication available today. Give them to him as gifts. Volunteer to read the books to him. Play the cassettes in the car when you're riding together. Or you can encourage him to establish close relationships with other godly men, and let him find his own third party.

There are lots of other ways men's and women's communication styles differ. For instance, I've had women tell me that their husbands don't look at them when they're discussing something. And further, he stays silent while she's speaking. He doesn't say *anything*. When two men are talking, we're usually *doing* something at the same time—reading the paper, watching a game, playing golf, or eating lunch. Most of the time we're side by side. We will be looking out the window, at the game, or at nothing in particular while we talk. Once in a while, we might glance over at each other and then quickly look away.

Women, on the other hand, will sit knee to knee if they can. At least they will sit so they can look at each other most of the time, and once in a while, they will glance away—just the opposite of what the men do. During the sharing, the women will give each other encouraging sounds along the way to make sure the other person knows she is into what's being talked about. Men are usually silent between their times to speak.

Therefore, when a man and a woman talk, if he's not looking at her or making encouraging sounds, she thinks he doesn't want to be involved or doesn't care. I always took Barb's little encouraging noises as *approval* of what I was saying, whereas she only meant to show interest. It was such a shock to find out at the end of my part of the discussion that she had another opinion.

I had the men's Bible study practice looking into each other's eyes one morning so they could go home and impress their wives. It was *so* uncomfortable. One guy said it gave him the willies, and I agree.

Focus on the Other Person's Needs

Barb and I just had an interesting discussion. It is Saturday around noon, and I've been working hard on this book as usual. It's filling all the cracks I usually have in my schedule of making a living, doing ministry-related projects, counseling, and keeping the home shipshape. Therefore, I have not been as available to her as I would like to be. I finished the rough draft of a couple of chapters, so I wanted to make a connection with Barb. I finally found her in the sewing room. She was ironing and listening to one of the prophecy tapes I gave her for our anniversary. She's teaching a course on the book of Daniel and is very much into learning about the "last days."

I said, "If you would like to do something—go to a movie or go antiquing or just go for a walk—I'm available."

She said, "I only have a few more things to take care of, and then I'm available. What would you like to do?"

I said, "I don't necessarily want to *do* anything, but I want to meet *your* needs in case you want to take a break or do something later this afternoon."

She said, "Do *you* want to go?"

I said, "I want to go if *you* want to do something."

After some more "he-said, she-said" conversation, I finally asked whether she had a *need* to do something.

"No, I don't have any *need* to do anything," she said. Then she asked if I needed to do something.

I said, "I'm here to meet *your* needs. I don't have any needs right now."

She said, "Neither do I," so I went back to my writing, and she started the audiotape again.

My focus was on meeting her needs. Her focus was on meeting mine. *That's* the way both our needs can be met, by focusing on the other person. This is one of the best-kept secrets about marriage—to spend full time focusing on, being creative about, and thinking about how you can fulfill your partner's needs. When you take him on as a project (and especially if he does the same for you), it gets your eyes off yourself, which is *exactly* what God wants, and He will bless your relationship because of your giving attitude.

The obvious question now is, "What if your husband doesn't take *you* on as a project?" Most of the time the man is causing the marriage problems. You might challenge me on this, but in my experience I would say that 90 percent of the divorces are caused by a man not understanding what his wife needed from him. On the other hand, I can only remember a few women who, from my outside view, were doing everything possible to meet the husband's needs. They were not following God's advice to approve and build him up, flirt with him, have fun with him, smile at him, adore him, admire him, and think highly of him. I realize it's hard to do this when your husband's a jerk, but in some cases it might be like Chesterton's statement that "Christianity has not been tried and found wanting—it's been found difficult and untried." Maybe you haven't given it your best shot. But if you honestly know you are doing everything you can, then you're doing everything you can. God will have to make up the difference, and He will. He will see to it that you are blessed for your effort.

I love how Barb's and my friendship has grown over the years. We're comfortable together. I want to make sure it stays that way, so I'm always looking for tears from Barb or a tense countenance just in case I'm involved in some way. We've even developed a type of shorthand communication that tells me how she is. Just last night, I came into the living room, and Barb looked as if she had been crying. I asked if anything was wrong. She nodded toward the TV. She was watching a movie. I asked her, "Cancer, dying, or someone run over?"

She answered, "Dying," and I went out to fix a sandwich, knowing all was well.

Please keep in mind that even after 40 years of being married, writing marriage books, and teaching relationship seminars for thousands of people, Barb and I *still* have to work and compromise in this special relationship called marriage. Barb still hopes that someday I will finally be able to communicate immediately without anger, say "Wonderful!" when told about the wedding on Saturday during the NFL play-offs, wipe down the sink, and pay more attention to details.

I know sometimes you have just *had it* with your mate's failures and shortcomings. If he would only be a little more like *you*, things would be so much better. But finally, you get back to the realization that there is compromise on both sides. And you *do* learn how to meet each other's needs a little more consistently as the years go by, though at times you simply hit the wall with your frustration at something he does or doesn't do, and it's okay. This is to be expected, worked through, and learned from. Then, after you've worked through the problem, understanding, friendship, mutual love, and respect increase and give you wonderful stories to tell to other people who are going through the same thing.

The key to handling marriage conflict is to have a lifetime commitment. You need to verbally say to each other that no matter what happens, you will not leave or seek a divorce. You *will* work things out, even though there may be times when you feel like walking away. If you don't have this type of commitment, one person can emotionally blackmail the other by saying, "If you ever say that again, I'm out of here." The one being blackmailed can never state real feelings for fear the other one will leave. When you have the foundation of "till death do us part," however, you can have conflict and resolve it in a healthy way.

Some of you reading this book have been divorced. You've already lived through what I've been talking about. Don't be discouraged, and don't look back at the What-ifs. If you've remarried, make sure you have made a lifetime commitment to your present mate. Then and *only* then can you have the type of interaction that solves problems rather than runs away from them.

One of the things that colors a man's communication is his deep need to be independent. Let's look next at how this affects his life and yours.

11

Preparing for the Super Bowl Takes Time

Barb and I love to watch "Capitol Gang," "The McLaughlin Group," "Washington Week," "Equal Time," "Reliable Sources," and those kinds of TV programs in our old age. I remember my grandfather always listened to Gabriel Heater and Walter Winchell. We had to be very quiet, and for sure we couldn't talk to him as he sat in his old rocker, glued to his radio set. So we sit glued to our TV sets as we see Fred Barnes, Mona Charen, and John McLaughlin give us the scoop on what happened in our world that week.

For most men, of course, the week prior to the Super Bowl every year is one of the most spiritually meaningful times in life. The game has been hyped every day in every newspaper, in every sports report on every national network and local TV station, and as well as on all the sports cable channels. There are 750 million people around the world all tensed up as the great day approaches, and this is as it should be. You wonder how we men can sit alone in front of the TV for hours on end, not caring to relate, but that's only because you don't appreciate the significance of the event.

Preparation is essential for us vicarious sports enthusiasts, so it's vital that we men have a TV visit with all 90 players making up the two teams as we ask them how they're approaching this all-important game. We need to talk to the coaches and learn about their strategy, both physical and mental.

After we talk with all the coaches, it's important to visit with the ball boys at the stadium to see what preparations are being made for the Gatorade shower for the winning coach near the end of the game. They have to hide those intentions from the coach until the last possible minute, so there needs to be quite a bit of planning and positioning to make sure it comes off right.

Then it's vital that we speak with some people on the street about what personal preparations they will be making for this special event. We want to know which brand of chips is "in" this year.

It's an exhausting week for all of us, but we must have this background before the big weekend arrives. Las Vegas prints the odds on which team is the favorite. All the newspapers have a tale-of-the-tape comparison between the two teams to look at the strengths and weaknesses. The team names are on the lips of all informed Americans as they begin to decide which of the teams they think has the best chance of winning and who deserves their support.

Then comes Saturday evening. This means we have only a few more hours of agony before we can see maybe one of the greatest events in the history of mankind, other than maybe the invention of the printing press and the discovery of fire. It also means that Al Hunt, Mark Shields, Bob Novak, and the rest of the Capitol Gang will bring us up to date on what's happening in the world.

Of course, the most important item on the panel's agenda is always covered first. So one Saturday night before the Super Bowl, Al Hunt asked Margaret Carlson, the only woman member of the august panel that day, who she thought would win the big game. She threw up her hands and said, "Who's playing?"

There, ladies, is the basic reason there is so much friction between men and women and why we don't communicate, even though we're all speaking English. Here was the most important event in the universe other than the Big Bang. Billions of our precious dollars had been spent promoting this critical phenomenon, *and she didn't know who was playing!* What planet had she been on?

I'm not saying all women are that deaf and blind to important events. I know there are women besides the players' wives and mothers who *love* to watch the Super Bowl. There's a woman in Chicago, one in Tokyo, one in London, and a real fanatic in Chico, California, but those are the only ones we know of right now, so is it any wonder so many marriages are on the rocks?

We men get so much abuse from women for wanting to watch sports on TV. What you women don't realize is that *it isn't our fault* that we look at so many games on TV. It's the *announcers'* fault—people like Keith Jackson, whom I heard talking about an upcoming Florida State-Miami football game. He called it "the game of the century." Now, who in his right mind would want to miss the game of the century?

And those promos for the upcoming Monday night football matchup yell at us, "Don't miss next week when the greatest contest since Moses versus Pharaoh takes place! It's Joe Montana versus John Elway! Exciting, bone-crushing action is in store as these two magnificent teams battle it out!" Then it's *blooey, pow, crash,* and sparks fly as the helmets hit head-on, and we have to catch our breath because of all the excitement and anticipation. What red-blooded, patriotic American is going to pass up Montana versus Elway? It glues us to our chairs as we await this once-in-a-lifetime event.

And it's not only important to participate in these Big Bang-like sports events at the end of the regular season; it's vital that we watch all the play-off games, too. It takes a lot of careful planning and energy to pull this off. I just don't think you women know what we have to go through. Usually, there are two play-off games opposite each other on different channels. This is where the gift of clicking comes in. A man needs to click back and forth between the games so he doesn't miss anything essential. For sure don't try to communicate with your husband during this critical stage.

If you *must* speak to him, I suggest you call from the doorway first to make sure he knows he has a wife. You could get hurt with all the jumping up and down and arm flailing he does watching the game.

Not only do we have to watch the play-off games, but we also have to see all the preliminary games during the season leading up to the play-offs. We need to see which baseball managers finally bring a faltering bullpen to strength.

In addition to all that, we need to keep track of what's happening in the *other* sports ESPN brings to us. We can't have the network spending all that money without our support. That means we have to keep up on the latest in the University of Wisconsin versus Michigan State chess championships, plus the archery battle of the decade between Ole Miss and Memphis State. We need to see how the Australians are coming with what they laughingly call foooootball. We can't make heads or tails of what's going on. Sometimes the player just stands there holding the ball. And sometimes the player just stands there holding the ball, and he's *creamed*. But it's important that we be more global-minded, so we watch it, even though we don't really understand what is going on.

Next we watch the England versus Spain soccer match, which is an important tune-up for the coming World Cup. Then we watch the downhill skiing finals in Norway; beach volleyball; a couple of tennis sets; an analysis of the upcoming

Indy 500 race; duck hunting; fishing in the Everglades; golf from Pebble Beach; and the monster truck smash in Enid, Oklahoma.

And here's good news for all four of you women sports fans: Someone has just announced a new TV channel that will play all the *past* sporting events starting with Spartacus versus Octavian in the Coliseum in Rome. That means every Christian versus lion and sword man versus net man; every football game; baseball game; tennis match; golf game; Indy 500; Daytona 500; Asheville 500; Nashville 500; Ponca City 500; every NBA final ever played; the greatest 230 boxing matches of all time in slow motion; the 50 best Mayan stickball matchups in history—all will be there for you and your husband to enjoy. And if you really want to be a good steward of the time God has given you, record some of the events and play them back on your VCR during commercials.

Barb and I worry about doing our marriage retreats on Saturday because all the men have to be dragged along by their wives, and they're not in a good mood. They tend to lash out at people, and you have to be careful. There are *always* important sports events on Saturday that the men are missing—critical games in the NFL, NHL, CFL, CNN, CBS, NBA, TBA, TBC, CIA, PDQ, OIC, and the Final Four. You know, I'm surprised we men have time to go to work with all the sports cable channels now. Just wait for the information superhighway, which promises to have up to 500 TV channels to choose from. Then we'll be able to watch the Absolutely Normal School's checker championships direct from the gym in Dubuque, Iowa; thrill with the Irish dart championships from one of the Dublin pubs; and faint from the action of the marble finals from Madison Elementary in Boston. I can hardly wait.

Actually, ladies, I think this portends a great danger for the human race. When we get 500 channels available, the men of the world will not have time to have sex with their wives because of all the sports and other important things on TV. That means the human race will go *kaput*—right down the drain. I hope someone can think of something to solve this crisis before it's too late.

Our competitive nature is one of the things that makes us men tend to be very independent. And sometimes our need for independence makes us defensive when you ask us to do something for you. There are two things working against you—two fears that are common to men. The first is the fear of failure, man's greatest fear. If he fails in any area of his life, he is destroyed. If he gets fired from a job, fails in his relationship with you, strikes out, drops the pass, or doesn't make his sales quota, he feels inadequate and defeated.

This is why a man doesn't like to ask for directions—he feels as if he has failed. He's going to do everything in his power to find the address on his own. So even when Barb suggests I stop and ask someone where we are, I want to keep the car moving in the general direction of where I think the address is. To stop and ask someone would be a sign of weakness. Besides, Barb has seen some wonderful neighborhoods she would have missed otherwise. Eventually, the Lord puts a halo over the right address, and we find our way. I surely don't need any help. If it takes a couple hours more than we thought it would, well, I didn't want to see the wedding anyway.

The second fear is one that Barb thinks men have, and that's a fear of being dominated by a woman. The reason I say "Barb thinks," is that I have not fully come to grips with this in my life. I've not had direct experience working for a woman boss, but as I imagine what it would be like, it seems like I would have worlds of respect for her and want to do everything I could to make her successful. She would no doubt have wonderful qualities most men bosses don't have. She would have her personhood intact, she would be working hard on her relationships, and her multiaware brain wiring would benefit me directly. I know some very strong women leaders, and I think I could serve them well. On the other hand, since I have never experienced this, I could have a blind spot, so I'll go with Barb's thoughts on the subject.

I do know, however, that in marriage relationships we men give you resistance, especially when you try to give us helpful little hints on how we should run our lives. And we sometimes take your suggestions as nagging when they involve the things on your to-do list we are not getting done.

Barb says men nag, too, but she calls it *badgering*. She says a man talks about something over and over until the wife finally agrees to do it, even though she may have doubts about it. Barb says I badger her when I want her to go along with one of my world-changing ideas and won't quit talking about it until she finally gives in. But how can I stop talking about an idea when it would benefit the whole world so much?

We spoke for a Sunday school class recently, and as part of our talk, we recommended that couples not make decisions unless both partners are in agreement. Afterward a young couple came up, and the woman was crying. It seemed her husband had always given verbal assent to the theory that they made decisions together, yet when she did not agree with him, he would keep at her and keep at her until she gave in, even though she still didn't like his decision. Barb told her she had been badgered!

Now, I need to explain why I'm in a no-win situation on this. Early in our marriage, Barb asked me not to surprise her with my goals and ideas. After thinking about her request, I realized that I usually thought about an idea for a couple of weeks, then sprang it on her at dinner and expected instant approval. I visualized her running around the table, swinging her napkin in the air and saying something like, "That is the most fantastic idea I've ever heard!" What I normally got back was a raised eyebrow, a catch in her breath, and a perception that I had just said "fire" in a local theater. It dawned on me one time that I was thinking about a wonderful idea for two weeks, and it wasn't fair to her to expect her to process my thoughts in just a few minutes at dinner.

When I had a world-changing idea I began writing her notes to give her time to think about it. The problem was, I seldom got my notes back, and I took that silence as approval. But Barb assumed that if she didn't get back to me, I would forget the idea.

Men's resistance to advice begins at an early age. Dave Valle, the Seattle Mariner catcher for many years, was one of the best catchers in the American League. One time Dave was trying to give advice on the finer points of baseball to his seven-year-old son, Philip. What a unique opportunity! To be tutored by a real, live professional baseball player. What boy wouldn't give almost his life for such an opportunity? But what did Philip say to his dad as Dave began giving him instruction? *"Dad, I can do it myself!"* Even at that young age, the mini-man doesn't want to be told what to do.

Our firstborn grandson, Cameron, is an example of why these male tendencies are designed by God and not created from the child's environment. When Cameron was nursing, his mom, Beverly, would look down at him with adoring eyes. But when she did this, he would *stop* nursing and *start* fussing. When she looked away, he was fine. He just didn't want any woman telling him how to *nurse*. It finally dawned on Bev that she was letting a couple-of-months-old male run her life, so she purposely *stared* at Cameron until he got the message and stopped his fussing. But it was quite a battle.

Cameron's dad, David, is into lifting weights and using an exercise machine. I made Cameron some little wooden barbells, and he would hold them up and make a sound like Tarzan, even though I don't think he knows who Tarzan is yet. I also let him push the button for our garage door opener. He pushes it and then with a shout points to the door going open, as if to say, "Wow, look what I did!"

Just this week, Barb and I were speaking to a women's group, and a mother came up to me afterward. She was perplexed because she and her teenage boys no longer had the friendship they had while the kids were growing up. She told about how they talked, had fun together, and for sure shared their lives. But now, all she got when she asked how school went that day was "fine." What had happened?

I tried to explain that they were now boy-men. Their hormones were kicking in and making them more independent. I tried to assure her that they would come back as friends sometime after their twenty-first birthday, but I still don't think she understands or accepts what has happened. She just said over and over how much they had "changed." Welcome to the teenage years, Mom. It happens every time. In fact, I'll bet Adam and Eve's boys Cain and Abel asked the sandal shop owner, "If our parents like these sandals, can we bring them back?"

They're an Independent Lot

First our moms experience our independence, and then our poor wives get hurt. I'm very sorry. You are so trusting and wonderful, and these qualities get you in trouble sometimes. You have a deep love for your husband. You have a nurturing nature designed by God. From time to time, then, you give him some suggestions to help him along life's highways and byways. You might say something like, "It's probably going to get cold. You might want to put on a sweater." "Are you really going to wear those blue socks with that brown tie?" "Don't you think you should take an extra handkerchief because of your cold?" You're not trying to dominate your husband. You just have a caring, helpful heart.

All of a sudden, however, he's defensive and might even be angry at being "told what to do." You wonder how you got in this mess just by trying to be nice. You need to know about his deep fear of being dominated by a woman and being put into an inferior position. This is not a conscious thought process. He doesn't plan to be a beast or to hurt you. It just sneaks up on him as he perceives you're trying to tell him what to do.

The same thing happens to Barb with repairmen. One time we spent $200 on our dishwasher because of this fear. Our dishwasher wouldn't drain properly, so we called the repairman. After he got the door apart, Barb noticed a toothpick had lodged behind the float and was keeping it open. She made the mistake of pointing this out to the repairman, and he tested *everything else* before he finally decided he might check to see if that had been the problem.

So here's a helpful hint for you: Never give a repairman the idea you know what's wrong. Use the "Elizabeth Taylor" principle. The more helpless you act in this situation, the more he will want to help, but he has to do it "his own self." Sorry, ladies, that's just the way we're made.

Is there any hope? Well, I guess I'm an example of the thousands of men who have learned to do it right once in a while after having been exposed to Jim Dobson, Gary Smalley, Tim Kimmel, and other marriage experts. But we have to be taught. That's a theme you've heard over and over in this book. There's no simple answer, but there is one thing I know, you can't do it by yourself. So don't even try or *you'll* be the one who suffers from your husband's independent nature, and that wouldn't be fair.

I don't mean to leave you hopeless. I know you probably feel like that sometimes during our discussions. Just watch for my references to a man's "third party," and by the end of the book, you should have a good idea of how to help in the assembly process.

I've talked about a wife not fully understanding her husband's independent nature. Now let's examine the home, an area where the *husband* is the one who doesn't understand what's going on.

12

Be Sure to Clean Before the Cleaning Lady Comes

I t was the morning of our thirty-ninth anniversary. I was up early and was working on this book. Barb came down to my office, we hugged, and then she backed up to me for a neck rub. We had given our marriage seminar for a church the night before; she had a big family dinner coming up; we were about to leave for a Pro Athletes Outreach conference; and she had her Tuesday Bible study to study for, so she was tense and achy. She said with a twinkle in her eye and a smile, "It must have been the 39 years of marriage with you that's causing my pain."

I quickly corrected her, saying her 59 years of *age* were doing it, and maybe our schedule. I could only remember two times when I caused her stress. One was back on June 15, 1973, and the other was on January 7, 1982. She has had a wonderfully stress-free life since then. However, some stress for *me* was about to happen.

I usually put the water on in the morning for coffee. If Barb isn't up by the time it's hot, I will also *make* the coffee. But this particular morning, I couldn't find the filters. Barb has two areas where she keeps supplies, in a large kitchen cupboard and out in the garage. I scoured the two areas, but no filters. So I ate my breakfast and was reading the paper when Barb came down. Then I told her we were out of coffee filters. She went over to the *cake mix* drawer, and there were the filters. That's not even *logical*. That would have been the *last* place I would have looked for coffee filters, but it seemed to make sense to her somehow.

In the process of making coffee, she asked if I was washing out the pot with soap before I made coffee. I can faintly remember a discussion of this topic some years ago, but it had not seared into my brain in any way. I always rinsed the pot with pure tap water, but I wasn't really aware that I had to do more. When she asked me about the soap, my eyes rolled back in my head. I became dizzy. I had this sick feeling rushing through my system. I almost fainted, and my liver began to quiver. I was suffering what many husbands experience. The medical term for it is "RO." It's a horrible sickness that causes great stress to a man's heart, kidneys, liver, pancreas, thyroid, stomach, large colon, lymph system, and brain stem. Usually it's fatal, but not always. The expanded name for this awful disease in the medical books is "Rule Overload"—RO for short. A husband can accumulate only so many rules, and then his brain goes *pow!*.

So I have started washing the pot with soap in the morning before I make the coffee. It usually takes me until noon to get all the suds out, but I don't have anything else to do anyway. Actually, we have joined the elite by serving flavored coffee. I'm sure you've heard of mocha and Irish cream for coffee flavorings. At our home, you have your choice of Ivory, Borax, or Dial, but at least the pot is clean.

I have a thick book of rules I have to follow to prove my love for Barb. Here are some of them:

Rule: Put dirty silverware in the dishwasher starting at the left.

I have no idea why this is so important to Barb. It might be because she's left-handed. I'm right-handed, and it would be easier for me to put them in starting on the right. In fact, it doesn't matter to me in the first place. I just drop in the silverware from eye level, like bombing from a B-17 in World War II, and marvel at my accuracy. Come to think about it, I've never tried to drop them from behind my back, so I think I'll try that tonight. Only a few knives and forks fall points down onto the kitchen floor when I miss, so the damage is minimal, but I put the silverware in from left to right because I'm committed to Barb.

Rule: Do not put plastic in the lower part of the dishwasher.

I happen to know how a dishwasher works, and the force is no greater on the bottom rack than it is on the top. You'd think the plastic was going to melt or something. This involves the fifteenth rule of thermodynamics, which I don't have time to explain here. Plastic is plastic; soap is soap; water is water. This rule makes no sense, but I do it because I'm committed to Barb.

Rule: Rinse dishes before putting them in the dishwasher.

Why do we go to all the expense of a dishwasher if we're going to do the dishes before we put them in? Sounds like a poor use of God's funds, but I go ahead and rinse the dishes because I'm committed to meeting Barb's needs.

Rule: Wash down your bathroom sink before the cleaning lady comes.

This is really a strange one. Why do we hire a cleaning lady if we're going to clean the house before she comes? Barb also does some vacuuming, dusting, painting, rewallpapering, and prying of the moss off the roof before the cleaning lady appears. I realize we wouldn't want her to think we actually *live* in the house. But I wash down my sink because I'm committed to Barb.

Rule: Don't wipe your hands on the towels. (Barb added in her editing "if your hands are not completely clean.")

As you already know, I was raised in the summers on a farm and worked on greasy farm machinery, and we always had what we called grease rags. The idea was to wipe the excess grease off your hands before going into the house to wash. I say "excess" because it would make no sense to get *all* the grease off or you wouldn't need to go into the house to wash! The role of a towel in the house is to help get the last remaining grease particles off your hands so you'll be presentable at the dinner table. We never knew we weren't supposed to get the towels dirty. That's why we thought they were there—to wipe our hands on.

I suggest a wife look at those beautiful dirt spots as proof of how hard her sweet husband is working for the family. But Barb's attitude is "Woe to you" if you get a particle of sand on the towel. The towels should be pure at all times. But how do we get the last vestige of grease off our hands if we can't use the towels? I use my pants instead of the towel, however, because I'm committed to Barb.

Rule: Take off your shop shoes before coming into the house.

Okay, I understand this one. You don't want microscopic sand atoms on the rug. But there's always the danger that the man will forget to put his work shoes *on* again when he goes back out to his shop after dinner, step on a rusty nail, come down with configurtigguritus, and leave a young widow with orphan kids. But if you want to take this risk, that's up to you. I just know I wouldn't want that sort of thing on my conscience.

Rule: Wipe off the table after you eat.

Why do we have a cleaning lady? She comes every Wednesday! Besides, it's a miracle I can even find the breakfast table. Barb has two or three types of plants, some candles, and some of the kids' pictures on it, and I have to move all that stuff before I can lay out my paper and enjoy my breakfast. But I wipe off the table because I'm committed to Barb.

Rule: Make the bed if you're the last one up.

Here's where I want to talk about the principle of "adjusting." I don't blame you for wanting things nice around the house. I understand perfectly that the home affects your self-esteem whether you work in the marketplace or not. The problem is, the husband is not as skilled as the wife in some of the home areas, and bed making is a good example.

In the early years, I would make the bed, and then Barb would give me some "helpful hints":"The sheet is dangling out the end of the bed," "The pillows go at the head and not the foot," or "There's a big lump in the middle." The lump would turn out to be the dog or one of the kids—piddling details like that. I would feel like a two-year-old: *I can't even make a* bed *right!* I found out she was just more into the details of making it right. We've now solved that situation. If I'm the last one up, I make the bed as perfectly as I know how, and then Barb can adjust it any way she wants.

Rule: Make sure the tie and shirt match.

I have no idea why my tie and shirt have to match. Besides, no one at work is going to notice, because most of the people there are men. But for some reason, Barb needs them to match. I found out about this need early on when I would come down the stairs to give Barb a good-bye kiss before work and she would *scream*—at least it sounded like a scream—"Is *that* the tie you're going to wear?"

That type of question is another thing that irritates me about Barb. There I am with my briefcase in hand, my sport coat on, kissing her good-bye, and she says, "Is *that* the tie you're going to wear?"

"*Yes,* this is the tie I was planning to wear. What's wrong with it?" Obviously something is wrong, or she wouldn't have asked the question. I wish she would just come right out and say, "That tie looks dumb," and I would go back and change. Since I feel stupid when I can't find the right tie, we went to an animal system. If I have an elephant on my tie, coat, shirt, pants, shorts, socks, and shoes, I can go to work. But if I were to don shorts with a *raccoon* on them, I would be the laughing-stock of Seattle because I wouldn't match.

Install such a system for your husband. I know he would appreciate a system that would eliminate this type of conflict at the breakfast table.

Rule: Don't wear pants with spots on them.

I think the spots tell a beautiful story. It says that I had a wonderful time with the grandkids the last time they were over. There's a bit of chocolate syrup, a smudge from a Tootsie Pop, some ink from the pen we drew pictures with, a bit of grass stain from the wrestling match, grains of sand from the sandbox, some moss from the swing set, and a little paint from the wooden animals we made in the garage. I believe that anyone seeing those spots would just praise God that here is a grandfather who's having fun with his grandkids. It should be a matter of adoration, not criticism, but I change pants anyway since I'm committed to Barb.

Rule: Be "sparkly" at weddings.

I offend so many of my young friends when I'm honest about weddings. I've already told you how my whole life screeches to a sudden stop when I go to a wedding. No longer am I working on God's goals to change the world through the book, video, or radio program on which I'm working. No longer am I accessible to the phone to help desperate people with marriage problems. No longer am I able to read God's Word and learn from it. No longer is *anything* possible except to sit in a hard church pew and suffer.

If they had any decent magazines there, things would be a

little better. About the most exciting thing I've ever found in a pew was a booklet on the Nicene Council's discussion of the dispensational ramifications of the apostle Paul's trip to Troas. I'm surrounded by the ponderous thoughts of the ages, and Barb wants me to "sparkle." She sees my body there but says that "no one is home." I do try to sparkle, but I fail more than I succeed at this, I'm afraid. And by the way, if you want to discuss the Nicene Council's thoughts, give me a call.

Rules: Don't spray the windows with water when bathing the grandchildren.

Don't use so much bubble soap in the grandchild's bath.

Put all the toys back after the grandchild's bath.

Mop up the four inches of standing water on the floor after the grandchild's bath.

I don't even need to comment on these. You can plainly see how illogical such rules are and how they take the fun out of life.

Rule: Put gas in Barb's car if I use it.

Barb and I both have our own cars. I use mine for work, and she uses hers mostly for family. When we ride together in her car, I usually drive, even though she's just as good a driver. In fact she's probably a better driver, but this is the way we're comfortable. We were driving somewhere recently in Barb's car, and she noticed that the gas gauge was nearly empty. She berated me a little for not getting gas.

"I never drive your car," I said.

She couldn't believe what she was hearing. "*Of course* you drive this car," she insisted. "That's what you're *doing* at this moment!"

I begged to differ. *I* was not driving the car. *We* were driving the car. I never drive Barb's car unless she's with me. Driving the car means to me that I drive it by myself, and I never drive her car alone. But I still got in trouble for not getting gas. It wasn't fair because I was being criticized for something I never do. Drive her car.

Rule: Don't cut anything out of the newspaper until Barb finishes reading it.

The problem with this rule is that we never remember to cut out the cartoon or article I wanted to save until after the garbage man has come and gone. Besides, most of the time, the other side of the article I want just has the Chicago hog prices or an ad for seeking enlightenment through crystals. I know these are not things Barb cares about, so I take the chance and cut them out before she reads the paper. I realize this doesn't fit with my total-commitment statements, but this is something I must do because we've lost so many wonderful items in the past. She's resigned to this fact, and I'm careful to show her the hog prices before I take the piece downstairs to my office.

I asked the men in the Bible study I teach whether they have rules. The next week each man rented a hand truck and brought in the boxes containing all the rules his wife had for him. One guy couldn't go into the living room because they might have company at any moment of the day or night and it had to stay clean.

Another man was violating the biblical "put the toilet seat down" principle you women are so fond of quoting. His wife then did a shameful thing: She put one of those fuzzy covers on the back so the seat would flop down automatically when someone was through. I've run into those at homes we've visited. Ladies, I don't think you know how awkward it is to stand there with one foot holding up the seat. We men are in great danger of losing our balance, hitting our heads on the bathtub, and making you widows. I suggest you just put the seat down if that's what you want. We're equal now.

One man had to turn his socks right side out before he put them in the hamper. I can't imagine why this would be important. One side washes just as well as the other. I asked Barb about this, and she said women are afraid that if they don't get them right side out, their husbands will wear unmatched socks to work; have one right side out and the other right side in; or wear both wrong side out. He just won't notice. But neither will any of the other men at his job, so what's the big deal?

One time I wore two different kinds of shoes to work. I simply don't have time to bother with piddling details like shoes. Evidently, Barb's concern with such things has something to do with a woman's image. If another woman sees me with two kinds of shoes on, Barb says the woman won't say, "Why didn't Chuck notice that?" She'll say, "Why didn't *Barb* notice that?" So knowing it's her image at stake, I try to be more careful.

Another man, when he helps his wife vacuum, is only allowed to vacuum backward—something about leaving footprints. Horrors if someone should leave a footprint in a rug!

Yet another man was forced to take the garbage out before dark because that was what his wife's mother always did. His wife didn't give any other reason. Her mom probably emptied it in the daytime so she wouldn't get bopped over the head by a mugger.

One of the guys had a rule "Don't use a bath towel to polish your shoes or your airplane" (he has a vintage plane). One time he used three towels on his shoes and airplane. Rather than squeezing the grease and oil out of them and putting them in the washer, his wife *gave* them to him for his shop. I'm not sure she had the right attitude in this case. He didn't mean to get them dirty; they were just handy.

A friend of ours, Ken Hutcherson, was working in the barn on his minifarm when his wife, Pat, made one of her infrequent visits. She came in and commented on how dusty his barn was. Fortunately, she didn't add "No dust in the barn" to her list of rules, but that was a close call. I can't ever remember being in a dustless barn.

Another man's wife cleaned up his workshop and said, "I just finished vacuuming, and I don't want you in there again!" Well, not really, but that's how we feel sometimes when our wives come to the barn or shop. We need at least *one* place where we can be comfortable. It doesn't have to be a big deal. Maybe you can give your husband a closet somewhere if he's not into farming, woodworking, or fixing cars.

That brings to mind, ladies, your critical nature when it comes to the things we need to have in the yard to make your lives better. As we drive down the highways and byways of our world, I point out to Barb the homes that are obviously the domains of wise and wonderful women: There will be 15 old cars in various states of disrepair out back. Some of you don't understand, but someday some car is going to be stuck on the freeway and will need a front left brake drum from a '62 Ford, and your husband will be able to help. He'll probably be able to share the Lord with the people, win them to Christ, and save their souls for eternity as well. See what you would prevent if you had made him get rid of all his cars? Just have him line them up a little more carefully. I understand completely why you don't like them in a jumbled assortment.

They're Not Rules: They're Guidelines

Barb was a little offended when she read my jokes about rules. (Well, at least they feel like rules to me.) She said they're guidelines for making a home run smoothly and efficiently and living in harmony with a wife.

I follow the rules because I'm committed to Barb, but there are some times when I feel a bit deflated by what I perceive as criticism. It's just one more time I haven't done something right around the house, and I feel like a failure and a two-year-old. It's not Barb's fault. She's just trying to manage a home, and one of the big obstacles in that process is *me*.

Actually, the whole thing boils down to my *reaction* to her "helpful little hints." She's beside the point. I'm the one who needs to handle the "criticism" and take it the way she means it. She doesn't say things to tear me down, even though I feel torn down at times. She just feels, as you probably do, that since my greatest goal is to serve and love her, I would be *grateful* for information that would help me do that better. She knows I'm committed to the relationship, so I also try to make sure she knows that I'm open to suggestions.

Because of a man's design, however, he won't always take a woman's suggestions in the way you mean them. That's because most men are basically self-protective—at least I am. Women are, too, but you temper it more with concerns about relationships. A man's ego is very fragile, and he can easily be destroyed. Barb doesn't understand my defensive reaction to her question "Can we talk?" because my response is usually, "Okay, what did I do *this* time?" Barb *hates* for me to say that. After she expresses that feeling, my next words are, "But I usually *have* done something wrong, haven't I?" She agrees this is true, yet for some reason she doesn't want me to say what we're both thinking.

How Do You Say, "Thanks, Honey!"?

One of the reasons your husband responds the way he does to your suggestions and helpful hints could be the way they sound to him sometimes: "Thanks, honey, for hanging the pictures, *but* they should be lower." "Thanks for loading the dishwasher for me, *but* the plastic goes on the top tray." "Thanks so much for making the bed when you're the last one up, *but* the pillow goes in the middle." All your husband hears is the *but*, and he feels like he's failed again.

You can soften this a bit by using the magic word *and* instead of *but*: "Thanks, honey, for hanging the pictures, *and* they would even look better if they were a little lower. What do you think?" "Thanks for loading the dishwasher, *and* the plastic won't melt if you put it on the top tray, okay?" "Thanks for making the bed when you're the last one up. That really helps, *and* it would look even better if the pillow were in the middle."

I know this takes a lot of energy, but creatively tiptoeing around your husband's fragile ego will pay many dividends. You'll even get some of the projects done around the house that will make you feel better concerning what it says about you.

We men do make some boneheaded mistakes. Most of the women I've talked to, however, just get bitter and try to undo the damage without saying anything. I suggest you make sure you tell your husband what he did, because otherwise he won't notice anything is wrong except with you.

I take a great risk of offending you with my next question, but I need to chance it because I want you to see a bigger picture than you may be looking at right now. I can only ask the question from my limited view as a man, so you'll have to temper it with your wisdom. Here it is: Even when your husband makes a dumb mistake, even though he never can remember to do something right, and even though you feel he *should* pay more attention to details or appreciate the home more, what do you *gain* from criticizing him? When you complain about what he wears, does, looks like, or eats; about whether he plays too much, works too much, comes home early enough, plays with the kids enough, is the spiritual leader he *should* be, talks to your mother enough, hates weddings, watches too much TV, slurps his soup, trims the wrong tree, or weeds out the flowers and leaves the weeds—what do you gain?

I know what you *get*. Defensiveness, silence, probably some anger, and withdrawal. He feels destroyed and inadequate and vows *never* to share his heart with you again. Then he goes to his shop or work to grieve. If having revenge is worth doing this to your husband, that's your decision, but I think you'll lose in the long run.

For just one week, why don't you program yourself every morning, with a little dot on the mirror where you do your repairs, to give your husband *nothing* but unconditional love that day? And if you blow it, ask for his forgiveness quickly. Do you know what I think might happen? He might feel so good that he just might begin meeting some of *your* needs. But remember, no expectations. He might not. He might just sop up your love like a sponge and want another week, giving you nothing in return, but that's okay. God will bless you for your good try.

And here's another project. Too many times women don't appreciate what their husbands are *not* doing, like *not* having an affair, *not* having an alcohol or drug problem, *not* beating the kids, *not* hating Christ, *not* working too much, and so on. So I suggest you list all the things your man is doing *right* and praise him for them. Many times a woman's list is long and her tears are real as she reflects on what she already has.

My goal in all this is for *your* needs to be met. But you can't do it through criticism, even if your heart doesn't have that as a motive. I suggest you try hard to catch your husband doing something *right* and praise him for it. This builds up, energizes, and encourages him and lifts his confidence. When you catch him doing something wrong and criticize, on the other hand, it tears him down, makes him tired, discourages him, and undermines his self-esteem.

Looking at this from your standpoint, I realize that my suggestion isn't completely fair, because there *are* some things your husband is doing wrong, and you would like him to change. Barb and I asked this question at a couple's retreat one time: "How can a woman give her opinion without the man feeling like a two-year-old, as if he has two mothers, as if he's being cut up and spit out, or as though he has failed *again*?" We discussed the problem at length and came up with the only answer we could. It's impossible—at least without a huge dose of the Holy Spirit operating within her husband.

Most men have never been taught how to accept what they perceive as criticism without becoming defensive. Your desire is not to hurt him. Your desire is to manage a home where you don't have to do all the grunt work—a home that will reflect who *you* are, that is well kept, with a pleasing atmosphere in which to entertain guests. Or maybe you don't want him to burp at public dinners or look foolish with the big gravy splotch on his tie. Or you want him to "sparkle" when he's bored out of his mind at some relationship deal like weddings or visiting the in-laws, where he is so much on display.

For sure there *are* times when God asks us to help each other with our blind spots, but at least in my experience, those times are rare. God seems more pleased when I pay attention to my *own* weaknesses rather than dwelling on the few Barb has. We're both better off if I praise her strengths and make sure she knows I'm on her team, supporting her in everything she does.

Now let's talk about one of the hardest things for a man to experience, and that's the aging of his once-hardened, trim, muscled body into a fat, balding, hard-of-hearing, tired, old shell.

13

My Health Alternatives to Poor Health: Suffer Three Times a Day, or DIE!

Those seem to be the only alternatives as I grow into my sixties. I have disadvantaged taste buds that were abused when I was a child, thus turning my life's path from broccoli, sprouts, soy cheese, Wheat Thins, celery hearts, and zinc pellets to potatoes and gravy smothered in butter; luscious thick, juicy steaks; biscuits and jam; pancakes with lots of syrup; juicy bacon and sausage; milk shakes; and rocky road candy bars.

It's not my fault, so I resent all the pressure to lose weight that I feel from certain members of my family, the media, and the nutrition nuts loose on the street. I've discovered I don't like anything that's good for me, and I love everything that will do me in. That's why I face the alternatives of suffering three times a day at meals or dying. I haven't yet figured out which would be best, though I'm leaning toward death.

There's a slight chance I'll find the secret to weight control one of these days. If I do, I'll let you know. And don't give me this "Don't eat so much" advice. As the tobacco folks clearly point out about tobacco not being addicting, overeating has not been proved as having anything to do with getting fat. There just isn't enough evidence, and until I'm given definitive proof, I see no reason to change.

I didn't plan to get so tired when I got old. I'm almost too pooped to write this chapter on aging and health, but it's important you know how devastating it is for a man to grow older, so I'll try to keep going. This is not to downplay your own battles with aging as a woman, but since a man's ego is so fragile, I think it might be harder on a man to get old. Maybe it's equal.

I'm sure no one looks forward to getting old and hurting and having to get tests all the time. I don't like all that probing, prodding, and running through the lobby naked in front of the visiting nurses' association on my way to the lab to give a blood sample. Nor do I like being asked to cough when I don't even have a cold. And there's always something wrong. I'm too fat or too stressed, my cholesterol is up, my triglycerides are down, my blood pressure is up, or my blood clots are down. I'm on a roller coaster and I'm a big mess.

And it's always hurry up and wait at the doctor's office. I went in for a physical recently, got undressed in the examining room, and waited for two weeks before the doctor showed up. The nurses put an IV in my arm and kept telling me the doctor was on his way. What do doctors know anyway that I can't find in the encyclopedia on my own? Physicals are a complete waste of time, and sometimes they hurt. And we men don't handle pain very well.

You'd think we would handle pain better since we "play hurt" in a football game, remove a nail that has just been driven through a hand, and wipe our bleeding noses on our basketball jerseys between free throws. I guess we have to be macho in those situations, but when our hangnails act up, we whine.

Speaking of pain, I'm so glad God has entrusted having babies to you women. You're so much more gifted than we men. Yes, we have an important part to play, and at great sacrifice of time and energy we participate in the conceiving process. But then we have to get back to work, knowing you'll do a much better job of having babies than we would. We don't have the right equipment or the patience to accomplish this great work for God, and besides, I understand it hurts. I'm sure if Adam had had the first baby, he might have said something like, "That's it, Eve! No more!" and the human race would never have gotten past go. Thanks, women, for doing such a great job in the birthing arena. Keep it up. We men worship the ground you throw up on.

About 1:00 A.M. recently, I woke up with a terrific pain in my side. I'm used to pain in my side since I eat a lot of chili, but somehow it was different. It never let up. No matter whether I stood, draped myself across the couch, or laid on the floor, it was a constant pain. I don't like to bother anyone with my pain, so I fought it for an hour or so before deciding to wake Barb. I tried to be macho, but by the time I got around to waking her, I couldn't stand up for the pain. She drove me to the emergency room, and I was checked in. Never having been in a hospital before, I had no idea what to expect, except I had heard lots of horror stories.

One of the first people to see my face attached to my suffering body said, "Oh, you have a kidney stone." I guess some other folks had been in with the same problem. I had heard of kidney stones, but I hadn't paid much attention, because that was something *other* people got.

That night at the hospital, they put me into one of those gowns that flap open in the back. I don't understand the medical profession's reason for that. All our important parts are in the front, and it seems dumb to leave the back open. What are they going to do, rub your back or something? Anyway, I lay on a gurney or whatever they call those table things, but no one seemed to notice that I was writhing in agony during my last few seconds on this earth. I guess no one else was having a problem that night, because the entire 1972 graduating class from Absolutely Normal, the nurses' academy, was also in the room. But no one was aware that I was gasping my last before falling off the gurney and dying.

Do you know what I think? I think all the women there (the doctor on duty was also a female) were excited that finally some man would know how much pain was involved in having a baby. I later met a woman who had experienced both kidney stones and babies, and she thought the pain was pretty similar. At least you women have a baby to bring home when you're finished, however. All I had was a big rock.

Finally, someone heard the death rattle in my throat, and the entire graduating class came over to put me out of my misery. I was amazed at how fast my modesty left me. They were putting in catheters, accompanying me to the bathroom, and holding my vomit dish for me, and I didn't give a rip. All I wanted was for someone to get me out of my pain. That's all I cared about. It was amazing as I look back on it.

I went through about 50 hours of agony before they finally gave me enough morphine to calm it, and that relaxed me enough to pass the stone before they had to blast. I just don't want to ever experience that much pain again if I can help it.

I have an old football injury: I was kicked by a cheerleader. No, that's not true; I was much too shy for that. I just liked the joke and thought I would work it in. Actually, I guess I did have a football injury. A few years ago, I had to have arthroscopic surgery on a knee that went bad all of a sudden. Later, when I attended my fortieth high-school reunion, I was talking to a man with whom I had gone to school beginning in the first grade. He said one of his memories of junior high school was the time I was playing football and wrecked my knee. I didn't remember it, but evidently that was what finally gave out. Now I can say truthfully that I had an old football injury. I don't say anything more than that. I just let people assume it was with the Chicago Bears or Green Bay Packers.

Then, just about my forty-fifth birthday, I noticed that all the restaurants we ate in were saving electricity by lowering their lights. That was ridiculous. Here we were with the cheapest electric rates in the nation, and the restaurants were going overboard in conserving energy. I finally had to start taking a penlight with me when we went to eat so I could see the menu.

At about the same time, I noticed my arms were shrinking, too. I used to be able to read a book just fine, but my arms weren't long enough to hold the book out so I could see it anymore. I fought that for a while and have no idea how I came to this next con-clusion, but one day it dawned on me—*I need glasses.* I couldn't believe it. Glasses were for *old* people, not kids like me.

But the evidence was overwhelming. So I swallowed my pride, went to the drugstore, and bought ten pairs of reading glasses. I put a pair in every bathroom, in every briefcase, in my office, and by my bed. That way I could just use them where I needed them, and not have to have a big glasses holder sticking out of my shirt pocket announcing to people that I was getting old. Then I found out that my daughter Beverly, who kept the books for our company, was getting restaurant charge card slips that were added up wrong. So I finally faced the fact that I would have to start carrying glasses when I went out to eat.

The first pair I carried *with* me was a Ben Franklin type that I would put on when I was teaching. I would read something, fold the glasses, and put them in the case in my pocket until the next time I had to read. Then I would reverse the process— back and forth like this for an hour. It didn't occur to me to just leave them on my nose, because I was convinced I looked stupid peering out over the top of Ben Franklin's glasses.

Finally, I went in to get my first pair of real glasses, but they turned out to be *bifocals.* That's when I *knew* I was close to the grave. The only person I knew with bifocals, besides all the grandpas and grandmas in the world, was a man who played piano at our church. His face was always looking at the ceiling when he played, but I guess his eyes were on the music straight ahead. Now I know what he was going through, because today I wear *trifocals* and don't think much of it. We men can get used to *being* old; we just don't like the process.

I *really* knew I was in the sunset of my life when I went to check out hearing aids. I was only ten years late in doing this. I was missing too much in life—like everything Barb said. And when we were out at a social event, I would nod when someone asked if I thought he was too fat. So Barb encouraged me to look into getting some hearing aids.

My situation is explained by one of my favorite jokes about old age. Two old men (my age) were walking down a path. One of them said, "Windy, isn't it?"

"I thought this was Thursday," the other answered.

The first one said, "I am, too. Let's go get a Coke!"

I love the humor of getting older, but it isn't really funny until you're actually *in* the sunset years of life. Then you can joke about it.

At last count, I've had three sets of hearing aids. First I tried one of the brands sold on TV. I called the number I saw on the screen and was told to go to an office downtown. A handwritten cardboard sign was taped to the door, and I was met by a guy in a white coat that still had his lunch on it. He brought out what looked like Edison's first hearing testing machine. I had seen one at the Smithsonian. It made some noises and hummed a bit, the man tsk-tsked with his mouth, and soon I was writing a check for almost $1,000. I think you can tell I wasn't really impressed, but I had to get some hearing aids so Barb wouldn't find a younger man.

The first thing I noticed with my new hearing aids was that there were lots of supersonic airplanes flying overhead. I found out later they were flies. The crash of a knife hitting butter was deafening. The sound of all the people in a restaurant blinking their eyes drove me crazy. I heard things I hadn't *missed* hearing. I was happier in my quiet world. What was Barb trying to do to me anyway?

Shortly after that, Barb and I were enjoying a quiet corner of a restaurant when this balloon artist came by and asked if we wanted a balloon blown up. I had a date with my four-year-old granddaughter the next day, and I assumed it would be one of those silver balloons with a saying on it, so I said yes. Almost instantly, I knew I was in trouble. She brought out some long, thin balloons that were used to make wiener dogs.

It took her 15 minutes to do the balloons, and I was in pain the whole time. She twisted, knotted, and screeched those tiny balloons as the agonized sounds coursed through my new hearing aids. Was this for real, or was I dreaming? We were trying to eat, but the woman wanted to make conversation while she was destroying what little hearing I had left. Barb and I almost embarrassed ourselves, because if we had made eye contact, we would have been snorting and guffawing on the floor, and that would not have been a good testimony to the balloon artist. So we looked at our food, which we couldn't eat because we might choke, and glanced up at the woman with approving smiles, hoping it would help her finish and leave.

The next time I had my hearing aids examined, the doctor exclaimed that it appeared that a rocket had gone through them, scorching the sides. I knew what it was, but I didn't say anything.

I wish I could magically go back to my youthful hearing, but I can't, so pray for Barb. It's hard to repeat every word you say during the day.

I was still fighting the problem of not being able to hear when one day when our grandchildren were visiting, Barb said "Stir the gravy" and I burped the baby. She put enormous pressure on me to get some new hearing aids. I went to our health co-op, thinking they would have all the latest in hearing aids. They decided the ones that were best for me resembled briefcases and sat on the back of my ears. They used six flashlight batteries, and it looked as if I had two pairs of ears. But since my self-esteem doesn't depend on how I look or what other people think, do you really believe I care about being thought of as a wimpy, weak-kneed, ancient, memory-disadvantaged fossil? You *bet* I do and so does every other man.

When my hearing started going down, my left ear went faster than my right. The doctors first thought it was because of all the years of Barb's opinions banging against the eardrum, but that didn't pan out since she's usually sitting to my right. The only other possible explanation was a brain tumor behind the ear. That didn't sound too wonderful, but I really was at peace with the Lord, assuming that whatever happened, He knew about it and approved. Radiation didn't sound like too much fun, either, and I wasn't looking forward to vomiting all day on Fridays after my chemotherapy.

I went to a clinic and had a CAT scan done, and sure enough, there seemed to be evidence of a tumor. To make sure, however, the doctors scheduled me for an MRI, which was a fairly new procedure at the time.

The MRI was a big machine with a long, narrow tube in the middle just large enough to accept a person's body. I had to have my hands and legs tied down and my head clamped tight so it wouldn't move. Then I was put into the tube with the ceiling just a couple of inches above my nose. I had a cold that day, and moisture of all sorts was coming out of my eyes and nose, but I couldn't do anything about it. I had to be in there for 45 minutes without moving anything. I had never been claustrophobic before, but about halfway through, I felt I needed to scream and get out of there. It was probably the worst agony of my life so far, and it was all mental.

Near the end of my time in the machine, an intercom voice asked me what they were supposed to be looking for. I told them a brain tumor. They couldn't find it.

It could have just been a mistake that the doctors saw a tumor on the CAT scan. Doctors are human, too. Or it could have been a miracle by God, which is something He didn't have to do. People die every day with similar things. But I praised His name for giving me a little more time to be on this earth with my family. I know there was a lot of prayer on my

behalf as I was going through this process, and I'm going to give
God credit that He really did answer all the prayers with a *yes*.
When I see Him face-to-face, I'll ask Him about it. It might
have been a smudge from the doctor's peanut butter sandwich
on the CAT scan, or it could have been God's miracle. Either
way, I learned a lot about how temporary life is, especially as we
get into the final third of it.

Probably the hardest thing I've had to battle on a continuing basis is the pounds that keep accumulating around my
middle. I agree with the person who said, "A waist is a terrible
thing to mind." I hate being overweight, but I guess I don't hate
it enough to do much about it. I did try exercise, because I saw
all the ads in the newspaper that showed thin, muscular men
and women who were exercise club regulars. I had always taken
the verses seriously that say, "Spend your time and energy in the
exercise of keeping spiritually fit. Bodily exercise is all right, but
spiritual exercise is much more important and is a tonic for all
you do" (1 Tim. 4:7-8).

I don't like to violate scriptural principles, but I decided I
really did need to get in shape. I couldn't afford to join the clubs
where all the beautiful people work out, so I chose to get fit on
my own by running. The problem is, I *hate* to run. There also
seems to be a division of opinion on this. Some people say the
only way to really get in shape is to run. Others say that it gives
you shinsplints, whatever they are, or that it pounds your joints
out of whack or makes your little toes fall off. Maybe the ones
who sound the warnings don't like to run either. In fact, I don't
really believe that anyone likes to run except for those few
human beings who have passed the six-mile mark in a single
run. They say that once you've managed six miles, something
snaps in your brain and you *like* to run. Some people have been
known to run—hold on to your bonnets—26 *miles*. They live
somewhere near Boston, I think.

I finally get up my willpower to exercise on New Year's Day
every year. Right after my second dessert and the football games
are over, I resolve to do 100 push-ups, 50 chin-ups, 75 sit-ups,

and a 10-mile run every day, and not to have any candy or pizza for the rest of my natural life. I faithfully carry out my vow for several days, and then I look in the mirror expecting to look something like Arnold Schwarzenegger. But every year at that point, there has been *no* change! So I decide to forget the whole thing and go out for some ice cream. Why would anyone endure all that abuse if it doesn't work? Barb has this ridiculous idea of starting off by doing one push-up, two chin-ups, three sit-ups, and running one city block, then working up from there over a longer period of time. But what does she know about the manly art of exercising?

About 10 years ago, I finally discovered the secret that was going to get me in shape. I got a four-position home gym that I could put in my basement. I had seen one in the store window downtown, and every model in the advertising pictures looked like Arnold, including the women, so I *knew* it would do the trick, and I bought one.

One slight problem: It wouldn't fit in the basement. I had forgotten to measure it. So I put it in the garage, but of course, you freeze your tootsies off out there. I decided to build a simple small house to hold this marvelous machine that would make me look like Arnold Schwarzenegger.

One slight problem: The hillside started to slip when the carpenters began to put up the simple small building, so they brought in heavy equipment from Alaska to pound steel telephone poles into the ground. Hundreds of cement truck loads later, I finally had my exercise house. It only cost what a regular house would, but think of the investment we were making in my health—preventing my heart attack, lowering my cholesterol, upping whatever needed to be upped, and lowering all the things that needed to be lowered. Barb would be the beneficiary.

There was one slight problem. When I got all those muscles from working out in my exercise house, I was worried that I might crush Barb as I took her into my arms. But I decided to deal with that later.

So I entered my beautiful exercise room, newly painted,

steady as a hundred cement trucks could make it on the hillside. There was nothing to stop me from looking like Arnold.

Just one more slight problem: I used the machine for a couple of days, I looked in the mirror, and again I saw *absolutely no change*. I had been gypped once more, ripped off by unscrupulous money grabbers. But I've never been able to take anything back to a store, so I still have the exercise machine and the exercise house, and that's where I store my bird seed. Works great.

Bird seed. Ah! That reminds me of food. I'm convinced that it isn't right or wrong to like or dislike a certain type of food. Personally, I've always hated cooked vegetables. My mother always said, "When you get into the army, you're going to have to eat your vegetables." Well, I fooled her. I got married and took Barb with me to the army, and she packed my lunch and fixed what I liked for dinner.

I know most mothers want their kids to grow up big and strong and not eat so many sweets or fast foods and instead eat their vegetables. I respect this loving concern, but too often there's a "should" involved that I resist. Most moms want to force their own tastes on the family. I can tell you truthfully there's not *one* cooked vegetable that I like. I eat most of the ones placed in front of me when we're out in a small group so the hostess won't feel bad, but I've never eaten one that tastes good. On the other hand, Barb cooks up a little rice with some vegetables and thinks she has gone to heaven.

Now, I believe rice should only be eaten in China, Japan, and a few other Asian countries. It should never be served in any other part of the world. Barb also loves other foreign dishes like broccoli, sweet potatoes, and stewed tomatoes. She still doesn't get the fact that I don't. Things hit the fan one day early in our marriage when I came home to empty the garbage that was smelling up the place, and it turned out to be some vegetable she was cooking. Boy, did I get in trouble! I received clear instructions that for the rest of my life I was to *never again* make comments on Barb's vegetables.

Barb and my son Tim decided to test to see if my dislike for certain foods like cooked vegetables was in my head or for real. Tim goes deer hunting once in a while and brings home venison. I have never liked venison. Not just the idea of eating Bambi, but the taste is too strong or something. Tim and Barb wanted to fix some venison in a new way, and they guaranteed I would like it. So they put some in a pan and cooked it and served it to me on a plate. I agreed to take a few bites to see if I liked it. And I did! It wasn't half bad! I was amazed. It tasted almost like PORK! It WAS pork. They just pretended it was venison, and they were so dejected. My taste buds didn't fail me. I gloated for a week.

Actually, Barb has been careful over the years to cook the things I like, but she's frustrated sometimes because she can't cook things she would like me to try. I do what I can to soothe Barb's feelings. For our last wedding anniversary, I gave her a subscription to the magazine (I can't believe there is such a thing, but I saw it with my own eyes) called *Veggie Life*. I guess it's not all that much different from magazines like *Motorcycles Today* or *Workshop Hints*, but I hope she keeps the fricasseed-eggplant-flavored-zinc-pellet snack recipes to herself.

There's another biblical principle that clearly indicates God wants us to eat in restaurants. It's 1 Corinthians 9:27, where Paul talked about how he treated his body. Some translations handle the verse correctly and use the word *buffet*. Paul buffeted his body to make it do what he wanted it to do. Now, I take Scripture literally. If God says do it, I do it. If God says don't do it, I don't do it. And here is a clear command to buffet our bodies, so I recommend Seattle's Edgewater Hotel's buffet on Sunday after church. Ivar's has a nice buffet at the Salmon House. I think even Benjamin's has a nice Sunday buffet so we can carry out this scriptural admonition. Don't bother looking up the Greek on this one; just take my word for it. This is one of my life verses, so I wouldn't want anything to mess it up.

Even our freezer reminds me of how old I' m getting. It's like a geologic record of our married life. Have you ever seen the sides of rock walls along the freeway where all the various layers of sediment have been put down over the centuries? On the very bottom of our freezer are several pieces of our wedding cake from 40 years ago, along with the first ground beef Barb ever fixed me. Then there's a layer of baloney and bacon I was able to bring home from my job at the TV station because they couldn't take food that had been under the lights back to the store. Next are a few snowballs Tim and Bev created in the first grade. Then our business got better, as shown by a layer of T-bone steaks and lamb shanks. Now that I'm semi-retired, we have ground beef, hot dogs, and microwave pizzas in view. We keep plowing the top layer so the geologic record is intact for future archaeologists who want to see how families lived during the twentieth century.

Instead of my going to the freezer all the time, Barb keeps wanting me to go on a diet. I've suggested a couple of diets, but she hasn't been too impressed. For instance, I tried the SeeFood diet; I see food and eat it. I also tried the Mount Everest diet; I eat food because it's there. Neither worked. I have started 327 diet plans that involved 5,390 fiber-filled "chocolate" bars that have about as much flavor as dental floss. In fact, my dental floss has *more* flavor. It's mint!

The Slim Fast diet didn't work, either, regardless of what they say on TV. I would faithfully have a Slim Fast drink and then have breakfast. I would sacrificially have a Slim Fast drink at noon and then have lunch. I would, with great pain, have a Slim Fast drink at night and then have dinner. I didn't lose one pound on this diet. The truth is, I *gained* weight. It's amazing what they'll let people get away with on TV.

People tell me I should change my eating habits. I hate that term. It was thought up by some skinny, oat-bran-loving fruitaholic who wants to inflict his standards on the rest of the known world. I realize I should lose some weight, but I surely don't want to *change* my eating habits. I want to *enjoy* my eating habits, not change them. What I want is an old Indian formula where I walk around a tree 16 times chanting, and on the seventeenth time I shrink to what the insurance tables think I should be.

I think I was born in the wrong century. If I were a contemporary of Ben Franklin, I would fit right in with my rounded features and be considered very successful. But it's hard to stay round with all the nutrition nuts like Barb on the prowl, so I may have to go against biblical principles and try to get rid of my excess weight, even though it's not my fault.

I'm sure younger people wonder if all the excitement fades from life when a person reaches the sunset years. I'm here to tell you there are many exciting things we could do at our age, but Barb is against them. I recently suggested we change sides of the breakfast table. We've been on the same sides for 40 years now, and maybe we could take a chance and spice up our life together a bit. Barb doesn't think our hearts are strong enough to stand the excitement. Or for a real kick, we could change sides of the bed, go to a new restaurant, or take a new shortcut downtown. So you can clearly see there's still a lot of excitement in store for you younger people as you get older. Oh, by the way, let me tell you a secret: It's a wonderfully comfortable time of life. I recommend it highly.

Getting old really isn't a problem except we men make you women repeat every word you speak during the day, and we don't take you out to the disco every night the way you wanted us to when we were young. We wake up the grandchild when we get up out of the chair because of all the groans and pops coming from our bodies.

I joke about getting older, but the thing I need to remind myself of over and over is that without my health, I can't enjoy my family, be active with my grandchildren, or feel like writing, studying, or speaking. My satisfaction with life at my age begins with my health. I don't know why that's so hard to remember. I blame my busy life for not getting enough exercise or resisting the juicy bacon, but it doesn't make sense to do all the secondary things first. The benefits of a healthy old age are beyond measure. Why do I resist doing the right things?

Most men in the country either have a health problem or fear having one. A man fears losing his physical prowess, his shapely body, his acute hearing and sight. Your husband may not tell you he's afraid, but he probably is. He may be so afraid he doesn't want to see a doctor and have him confirm what they already suspect—he's getting older. He won't cooperate with your plan to feed him nutritious food, and he certainly won't take part in any exercise more strenuous than clicking the TV remote. This is so frustrating for you. You want to keep him around, and work so hard at trying to get up on a vitamin program and fixing special nutritious meals that are often rejected. I tease about food tastes, but as creative as Barb is, I have never tasted one low-fat, low-calorie, or low-sugar item that didn't taste like sawdust to me. I guess I get back to where I started. My only alternatives are to suffer three times a day or die.

I think I have pretty well covered the things in a man's makeup that might be mysterious to you as a woman. But as I look back, I don't think I have given you as much hope as I would have liked to. So much depends on whether Jesus Christ is at the center of your husband's life and whether he has another man he trusts who can come into his life to act as his mentor and teach him how he can meet your needs.

There is one thing you might be able to do on your own, and we'll talk about that next.

14

When You Release Something, Sometimes It Comes Back

I've told you about some of the power struggles my son Tim had when he was in school. He was not a bad kid in any sense of the word. He was just different, and I had never been taught that being different was okay. He really didn't give us an ounce of trouble except in his resistant attitude. His choices of friends and hours were also very difficult for us to accept.

When Barb and I decided to release him to God as I've told you in chapter 4, God began to work in his life. Tim began to let us know where he was, where he was going, who he was with. By releasing him to God's care, we gained back what we were losing.

I was having lunch with a young media friend, and I asked

him how everything was going at home. He said, "Great," except that his wife wanted to go on vacation to Phoenix in August. He had put his foot down. It would be way too hot, and besides, they couldn't afford it. He and his wife were having some heated discussions over this subject.

Then he made the common mistake of asking for my advice. I suggested that since his wife was his highest priority, other than his relationship with Jesus Christ, he should make arrangements to go to Phoenix in August. And he should be sure to take lots of T-shirts in case he sweated more than usual. I further suggested he remind his wife that she was the most important thing in his life after his relationship with the LORD. I added, however, that he probably would not have to go to Phoenix.

He didn't quite understand that last part, but he decided to take my advice. He sent a note a few days later to report that they were *not* going to Phoenix in August. His wife thought it would be too hot, and they really couldn't afford it anyway.

They had had a power struggle going. He was insisting they were not going to Phoenix in August. She was resisting him and was determined that they *were* going. When he released her, she did the right thing.

Another couple comes to mind. The man told me he was miserable. His wife had left him and was dating someone else. He was trying hard to get her back, but he was smothering her with his requests and begging. The first thing I suggested was that he needed supernatural power to get through this problem, and I introduced him to Jesus Christ.

He became a Christian, began releasing his wife to the Lord, and stopped trying so hard to get her back on his own. He focused on being the man *he* should be rather than on what she was doing wrong. She saw this change in him and was open to coming to a party in our home.

I guess she noticed we didn't wear our hair in a bun, walk around with our hands folded, or wear a big wooden cross and a flat hat the way religious folks do on TV. We looked and acted almost normal and even ate pizza! It wasn't long before she responded to this new spirit she was feeling from her husband, and they came to me hand in hand one day and announced they had gotten back together. Later the wife became a Christian, too. They have conflicts to this day. Barb and I do, too. But now they have the Lord to give them insights into how to work out a marriage relationship.

Wives can and sometimes must release husbands, too. I had lunch with a young woman whose folks have been family friends for many years. We've seen her grow up, so she is, in a sense, my daughter. She struggled with how different she and her husband were, and she gave me some examples.

First, he's more of a dreamer and entrepreneur than she is. He was trying to run his own business, but it wasn't going well. She wanted him to get a "real" job but couldn't bring herself to tell him directly. Her salary was paying most of the bills, and he seemed so "down" most of the time. I explained to her that much of a man's self-esteem comes from what he does. Also, men tend to look further up the road than most women do, especially the dreamer types.

What usually happens is that the man says, in effect, "In two years this thing is really going to click, and we're going to be successful."

His wife says, "But how are we going to eat tomorrow?"

He responds, "Well, I don't know about that, but I know that in two years this thing is going to really work out well."

The advice I give a husband at this point is to go out and get *any* kind of job, whether it meets his career goals or not. The purpose is to stabilize the family finances, and then when that's going well, he can work on his dream.

One problem in this case was that the woman's husband didn't feel as much financial pressure as she did, because she had assumed responsibility for that area. It was an out-of-sight-out-of-mind thing for him. *She* was handling the bills and getting all stressed out as she saw that their outgo was more than their income and they were dipping into savings. This fits with the way a man thinks. It's called no-news-is-good-news. If his wife isn't crying or creating a crisis by saying, "Let's talk," he thinks his marriage is one of the best in the world and his wife is as happy as a June bug. The wife *must* say, "Can we talk?" when things need to be resolved.

If you're in the same situation with finances, I suggest you say something like this: "Sweetheart, I think I've taken way too much of the responsibility for the finances. Would you forgive me? God has asked *you* to provide for the family, and I've been getting all uptight about paying the bills when the money is in short supply. You've had no way to know what our situation is. Therefore, I'm turning over all the finances to you. I still want to be your teammate in the financial area, and I know neither of us will make independent financial decisions, but from now on you're in charge of the day-to-day finances. If you want my opinion on something regarding our finances, just ask."

Some of you just fainted! "You mean turn over the finances to that spendthrift, irresponsible husband of mine?" I acknowledge the risk; I'm sure there are husbands who might take advantage of this arrangement. But my experience has been that when the wife steps back from paying the bills, God puts pressure on the husband to go out and get a job that meets the family's needs. Besides, it appears to me that the only alternative to this is to become bitter, uptight, and resentful about whether the family is going to make it financially. I suggest you put your husband in God's hands and ask Him to work in his life to motivate him to do the right thing.

Then when the bill collectors come to your home or call you, you say, "Oh, just a minute, you want my husband. I'll get him for you." You have a free spirit because you've given the situation to your husband and God. You can sleep nights and have a cheerful, loving attitude, content in the knowledge that the problem is God's, not yours. He has committed Himself to meeting your needs, and you can count on Him.

Yes, a few uncaring men out there would let the family suffer because of their irresponsibility. But of all the thousands of men I've met, none come immediately to mind as someone who would purposely harm his family in any way. Most of the time, no one has ever taught him what he needs to do to be a responsible provider. Your husband needs another man, a tape, or a book to come into his life and teach him what you need.

All of us try to make the other person into someone just like us. God wants us to release others to be who they are, not who we would like them to be. With a man, the more you press and criticize and expect, the more you'll push him away. Sometimes he gets to the point where he knows he will fail in your eyes regardless of how hard he tries, so why try at all?

The Secret for Transforming Your Marriage

If your husband is leaving you emotionally destitute, I suggest you release him and let God put the pressure on him to return. After all, God is more concerned about your marriage than you are. Picture your husband as disadvantaged and not able to control himself. Mentally see him in a wheelchair, especially a non-Christian husband. He simply doesn't have the supernatural ability to do the right thing. In your prayers, ask God to bring along someone your husband will respect who can help him trust Jesus to take over his life.

If your husband is a Christian, ask God to bring someone into his life who will teach him what the Bible says about what a husband is to be and do for his wife. Seek out a man who's involved in a small-group men's Bible study, and ask him to invite your husband.

Either way, your role is mostly to be an observer. The Bible says that if a non-Christian spouse wants to leave, let him. But usually what happens is that the man is so taken by his wife's quiet and gentle spirit when she does things God's way and releases him that he's attracted back to her. Sometimes the husband does leave. It surely is not guaranteed that he'll stay. However, it's unusual for a man to not be drawn to his "new" wife.

This doesn't mean you stop giving your opinions and become a doormat. It just means that after you've tried everything you know how to do to get his attention or help him change, you release him to God. Remember, He puts on better pressure than you do.

If your husband never picks up his socks, never becomes interested in spiritual things, or never keeps the flower beds weeded, release, accept, serve, and minister to your husband without trying to change him.

This is where you need the fruit of the Spirit, meekness. That doesn't mean weakness but strength under God's control. It's a serenity of spirit that accepts everything that comes into our lives as being allowed by God, whether we think it's good or bad. This enables us to go *through* trials in a God-honoring way. We can look at trials this way because we know He rules over all and is in control of every situation. He uses trials to mature us, to make us complete, and to mold us into the image of His Son.

Now someone might ask, "What if I don't release him?" You don't have to, but I believe you would then be on your own. God would go to Korea or work in Africa. Since you don't want Him to be involved in the process, He will let you do it yourself. He has lots to do. The problem is that BOTH you and God can't be involved at the same time. My recommendation is to let God handle your husband. I think He would do a better job.

I hope you haven't been too frustrated on our journey through a man's mind. I realize most of the journey was a trip through *my* mind. I think, however, that I'm typical enough that you'll see some similarities between me and the men in your life, and hopefully I've helped you understand them better.

Just keep in mind that your husband will *never* be like you, and you'll never be like him. God did not make a mistake designing you so differently from each other. That's His plan for most couples. Don't think you're weird if you're similar, however; just consider yourselves rare, and realize this doesn't mean you won't have conflicts. You'll just have different *kinds* of conflicts compared to couples who are so unlike each other.

Another question. What if you release your husband to God,

but he isn't open to change right now? He resists both you and God. Here are some things you can do on your own while God works out the timing of getting your husband's attention.

Find or create a support group for yourself. I've mentioned that Barb teaches this marvelous Bible study material written by Kay Arthur called "Precept Upon Precept." More than 100 women from all sorts of churches gather every Tuesday morning to study the Bible and support each other. It's life changing. Within the group are many women whose husbands are not supporting them at home. Just finding someone else who's going through the same situation is therapeutic.

If you can't find an existing group, start one of your own. If you're not working outside the home, find three or four other women in the same situation, and meet in homes for fellowship, prayer, and Bible study while the kids are in school. If the kids are small, chip in and hire a baby-sitter, or trade baby-sitting with other young mothers. You don't need the gift of teaching to do this. Just read through a book of the Bible, picking out practical helps for everyday living. Or get a book on marriage, child rearing, depression, anger, or stress, and have everyone read a chapter and be prepared to report on the things that touched them the most.

If you're working in the marketplace, find a restaurant with a backroom, and develop a relationship group during your lunch hour. There's a danger in this, of course. You could begin enjoying the small-group fellowship so much that you wish you didn't have to go back to work. So have a mobile phone handy in case you're a little late getting back. The only skills you need are the ability to call a restaurant and reserve a table in the backroom, plus the driving ability to get to the restaurant. The rest is automatic as God works through you and everyone else in the group.

If you have a fairly harmonious marriage, a small group would be a great way to reach out and help others who might be going through relationship struggles. If you have a horrible marriage, it will be a way for God to give *you* comfort as you share with other people the principles of being a godly wife in spite of what your husband is doing.

It's so easy to put your eyes on your mate and focus on his shortcomings. It's so hard to put your eyes on yourself and make sure you're fulfilling the biblical ideal for a godly wife. It's also extremely difficult for a wife to release her husband when he's not meeting her needs, is not interested in growing or in spiritual things, doesn't want to work on the marriage, or expects her to be his slave as he goes through his day. But she must confront him with what he's doing ("Can we talk?") and then leave the results to God. Contentment depends on our focus and heart attitude, not on circumstances.

I love the story about the woman with a husband who did the bar scene every evening until the wee hours. As he was talking to a couple of his buddies one morning at about two o'clock, he was boasting that he could go home and wake up his wife, and she would cook them breakfast and not complain.

"Sure, sure," they said.

So they all got into his car and went to his home. He awakened his wife and told her what he wanted. She put on a robe, went downstairs to the kitchen, and fixed them a sumptuous breakfast. All the while she had a sweet attitude and even looked as if she were enjoying herself.

Later one of the men took the wife aside and asked how she could do so much for them without at least a few complaints.

She explained, "Well, you see, I'm a Christian, and because of my relationship with Jesus Christ, I will be spending eternity in never-ending heavenly bliss. But my husband is not a Christian, so I'm trying hard to make his experience on earth as pleasant as possible, because this life is the best he'll *ever* experience."

A story is told of a young girl who needed a blood transfusion. Her brother was asked if he would give her some of his blood. After thinking a few minutes, he said with trembling lips that he would. As his blood was being drawn, the little boy looked up with tears in his eyes and asked the doctor, "When do

I die?" He had been willing to give up his life for his sister. You're not ready to live until you are ready to die to yourself.

You can transform your marriage all by yourself just by being the mate God wants you to be. There's a lot to learn, but you'll make progress with God's help. I know it sometimes feels as if there's no hope, but I like what Winston Churchill said to the British people during the German bombing of London in World War II: "This is not the end. This is not even the beginning of the end, but it could be the end of the beginning."

I hope that by now you've felt my heart of love and concern for you as a woman. We've agreed that your man causes many of your problems, and we've talked about some ways he can be taught what you need from your relationship. As I've repeated over and over, men have never been told about those needs. Most churches are doing a terrible job preparing men for marriage. Schools barely mention the subject. Fathers are usually not good role models because *they* weren't taught by *their* fathers. The pastor isn't very often a good role model, either, because even if he has problems, most of the time he feels he can't reveal them to the "sheep." One thing that helps is all the people who have learned from their mistakes. These lessons have been learned by going through the problems, not by just reading a book or trying to get out of problems. I'm uneasy listening to teachers who present principles that haven't been filtered through their lives to see if they work. I've read several "revised" books from authors who wrote their first books right out of seminary, and then started having their own kids, dealing with their own marriages, or trying to forgive or bless enemies, only to find things were more complicated than they were taught. However, if the problems you and I go through change just *one* other life for eternity, they're worth enduring.

I've always wished there were a training camp for a man so he could learn to meet a woman's needs better. There he could meet his third party. As I've emphasized over and over in this book, this third-party influence is critical as God goes about His assembly process with your husband. And now my dream is being realized, because more and more organizations around the country are teaching men how to be godly husbands and fathers. Some of them are Focus on the Family, with Dr. James Dobson; Today's Family, with Gary Smalley; Generation Ministries, with Tim Kimmel; Family Life seminars sponsored by Campus Crusade; Precept Upon Precept studies, including the "Marriage Without Regrets" course by Kay Arthur; and the exploding Promise Keepers ministry that I think just may be *the* organization that will save our culture from destruction. Hundreds of thousands of men are being trained to be husbands and fathers, and the ministry is growing so fast it's overwhelming to the staff. What a nice problem to have—so many men interested in learning how to be God's man for the family!

As a wife, anything you could do to encourage your husband to go to a Promise Keepers conference would be to your benefit. Here's how you can get information on this special ministry:

Promise Keepers
P.O. Box 18376
Boulder, CO 80308
(303) 421-2800

You're going to die when I tell you the thought that went through my mind about getting your man to a Promise Keepers conference. It's a recurring theme in this book, much to your dismay. But you can get your husband to go by making up a little card with numbers around the edges. Next, get a paper punch at the drugstore and make a deal with your husband. If he'll go to Promise Keepers, then after he gets home, he can present the card to you at any time, day or night, and you'll punch a number and instantly go to bed with him for a romp in the hay. I'm laughing because I just ran across a note from my editor, Gwen, that says, "What did you expect a man to suggest?"

If you're fairly young, you could have 20 to 30 numbers on your card. If you're a little older, eight to ten would be about right. You need to be careful of your husband's heart. But your "sacrifice" just might enable Promise Keepers to change his life, and thereby yours, for eternity.

Oh, by the way, if your husband has already GONE to Promise Keepers, make the punch card retroactive to remind him how grateful you are that he went.

It's going to take some time for God to change your husband, and there will be some tears. But when the tears come during your husband's assembly process, here is one of my favorite psalms to consider: "You have seen me tossing and turning through the night. You have collected all my tears and preserved them in your bottle! You have recorded every one in your book" (Ps. 56:8).

This implies to me that someday in eternity, the Lord is going to take us aside individually, draw a bottle out of His pocket, and explain the reason for every tear we have ever shed. I love the thought that God knows about and counts our tears. He's not some doddering old Santa Claus rocking on a cloud somewhere, incapable of giving meaning to our lives. I am His *son.* You are His *daughter.* And together we'll inherit everything He has prepared for His Firstborn and enjoy the eternal bliss He has waiting that goes beyond anything we can imagine—and I can imagine some pretty wonderful things.

I'd like to leave you with a prayer that comes from the depths of my heart:

When I think of the wisdom and scope of his plan I fall down on my knees and pray to the Father of all the great family of God . . . that out of his glorious, unlimited resources he will give you the mighty inner strengthening of his Holy Spirit. And I pray that Christ will be more and more at home in your hearts, living within you as you trust in him. May your roots go down deep into the soil of God's marvelous love, and may you be able to feel and understand, as all God's children should, how long, how wide, how deep, and how high his love really is; and to experience this love for yourselves, though it is so great that you will never see the end of it or fully know or understand it. And so at last you will be filled up with God himself. Now glory be to God, who by his mighty power at work within us, is able to do far more than we would ever dare to ask or even dream of—infinitely beyond our highest prayers, desires, thoughts, or hopes (Eph. 3:14-20).

With God's love,

Chuck Snyder
P.O. Box 22696
Seattle, WA 98122

Resource List

ADRENALIN AND STRESS
  Hart, Dr. Archibald D. Waco, TX: Word, Inc., 1986.

THE ART OF UNDERSTANDING YOUR MATE
  Osborne, Cecil. Grand Rapids, MI: Zondervan, 1970.

BEYOND ASSERTIVENESS
  Augsburger, David and John Faul. Waco, TX: Word, Inc., 1980.

THE BIRTH ORDER BOOK
  Leman, Dr. Kevin. Grand Rapids, MI: Fleming H. Revell Company, 1984.

THE BONDAGE BREAKER
Anderson, Neil. Eugene, OR: Harvest House 1990.

BORN AGAIN
Colson, Charles W. Grand Rapids, MI: Fleming H. Revell
Company, 1977.

CELEBRATION OF MARRIAGE
Wright, H. Norman. Eugene, OR: Harvest House, 1983.

THE CHRISTIAN USE OF EMOTIONAL POWER
Wright, H. Norman. Grand Rapids, MI: Fleming H. Revell
Company, 1974.

CONTROL YOURSELF.
Kehl, D. G. and Robert N. Bramson, M.D. Grand Rapids,
MI: Zondervan, 1982.

DEPRESSION
Baker, Don and Emery Nester. Portland, OR: Multnomah,
1983.

DISAPPOINTMENT WITH GOD
Yancey, Philip. Grand Rapids, MI: Zondervan, 1988.

THE EDGE OF ADVENTURE.
Miller, Keith and Bruce Larson. Waco, TX: Word, Inc.
1974.

FEELING FREE
Hart, Dr. Archibald D. Grand Rapids, MI: Fleming H.
Revell Company, 1979.

FREE TO BE THIN
Chapian, Marie. Minneapolis: Bethany Fellowship,
Inc., 1979.

THE FIVE LOVE LANGUAGES
Chapman, Dr. Gary. Chicago: Moody Press, 1992.

THE GIFT OF FEELING
Tournier, Paul. Atlanta: John Knox Press, 1979.

HEALING LIFE'S HIDDEN ADDICTIONS
Hart, Dr. Archibald, Ann Arbor, MI: Servant Publications, 1990.

HELP! I'M A PARENT
Narramore, Bruce. Grand Rapids, MI: Zondervan, 1972.

HELPING THE STRUGGLING ADOLESCENT
Parrott, Dr. Les, III. Grand Rapids, MI: Zondervan, 1993.

THE HIDDEN VALUE OF A MAN
Smalley, Gary and John Trent, Ph.D. Colorado Springs, CO: Focus on the Family, 1992.

HIDE OR SEEK
Dobson, Dr. James C. Grand Rapids, MI: Fleming H Revell Company, 1974.

HIS IMPRINT, MY EXPRESSION
Arthur, Kay. Eugene, OR: Harvest House Publishers, 1993.

HOW TO GIVE AWAY YOUR FAITH
Little, Paul E. Downers Grove, IL: Inter-Varsity Press, 1966.

HOW TO BEAT BURNOUT
Minirth, Frank, M.D.; Don Hawkins Th. M., Paul Meier, M.D.; and Richard Flournoy, Ph.D. Chicago: Moody Press, 1986.

THE HURTING PARENT
Lewis, Margie M. Grand Rapids, MI: Zondervan, 1980.

THE HYPERACTIVE CHILD
Martin, Grant Ph.D. Wheaton, IL: Victor, 1992.

IMPROVING YOUR SERVE
Swindoll, Chuck. Waco, TX: Word, Inc., 1981.

INCOMPATIBILITY: GROUNDS FOR A GREAT
MARRIAGE
Snyder, Chuck and Barb. Sisters, OR: Questar, 1988.

INTENDED FOR PLEASURE
Wheat, Ed, M.D. and Gaye Wheat. Grand Rapids, MI:
Fleming H. Revell Company, 1977.

LIFE-STYLE EVANGELISM
Aldrich, Joseph C. Portland, OR: Multnomah Press, 1981.

LIVES ON THE MEND
Littauer, Florence. Waco, TX: Word, Inc. 1985.

LORD, I WANT TO KNOW YOU
Arthur, Kay. Sisters, OR: Multnomah Press, 1992.

LOVE LIFE FOR EVERY MARRIED COUPLE.
Wheat, Ed, M.D. Grand Rapids, MI: Zondervan, 1982.

LOVE MUST BE TOUGH
Dobson, Dr. James C. Waco, TX: Word, Inc., 1983.

MAKE ANGER YOUR ALLY
Warren, Neil, Ph.D. Colorado Springs, CO: Focus on the
Family Publishing, 1990.

MAKING STRESS WORK FOR YOU
Ogilvie, Lloyd J. Waco, TX: Word Inc., 1984.

THE MAN IN THE MIRROR
Morely, Patrick A. Brentwood, TN: Wolgemuth & Hyatt,
1989.

MANAGING YOUR TIME
Engstrom, Ted W. and R. Alec MacKenzie. Grand Rapids,
MI: Zondervan, 1967.

THE MARRIAGE BUILDER
Crabb, Lawrence J., Jr. Grand Rapids, MI: Zondervan, 1982.

MEN AND MARRIAGE
Gilder, George. Gretna, LA: Pelican Publishing Company, Inc., 1986.

MEN AND WOMEN
Crabb, Larry Grand Rapids, MI: Zondervan, 1991.

MEN ARE FROM MARS; WOMEN ARE FROM VENUS
Gray, John Ph.D. New York: HarperCollins, 1992.

MEN IN MID-LIFE CRISIS
Conway, Jim. Elgin, IL: David C. Cook, 1978.

OVERCOMING ANXIETY
Hart, Dr. Archibald. Dallas: Word, Inc., 1989.

PARENTING ISN'T FOR COWARDS
Dobson, Dr. James C. Dallas: Word. Inc., 1987.

PARENTING WITH LOVE LIMITS
Narramore, Bruce. Grand Rapids, MI: Zondervan, 1979.

PERSONALITY PLUS
Littauer, Florence. Grand Rapids, MI: Fleming H. Revell, 1983.

THE PILLARS OF MARRIAGE
Wright, H. Norman Ph.D. Ventura, CA: Regal Books, 1979.

THE PLEASERS
Leman, Kevin Ph.D. Grand Rapids, MI: Fleming H. Revell, 1987.

POINT MAN
Farrer, Steve. Sisters, OR: Multnomah Press, 1990.

POWERFUL PERSONALITIES
Kimmel, Tim. Colorado Springs, CO: Focus on Family
Publishing, 1993.

THE POWER DELUSION
Campolo, Anthony. Wheaton, IL: Victor, 1983.

PRECEPT UPON PRECEPT
Arthur, Kay. Chattanooga, TN: Reachout Bible Series.

THE PSYCHOLOGY OF COUNSELING
Narramore, Clyde M., Ed.D. Grand Rapids, MI:
Zondervan, 1972.

RECONCILABLE DIFFERENCES
Talley, Jim. Nashville: Thomas Nelson, Inc., 1985.

RELEASED FROM BONDAGE
Anderson, Neil. Nashville, TN: Here's Life Publishers,
1991.

SAY IT WITH LOVE
Hendricks, Howard G., and Ted Miller. Wheaton, IL:
SP Publications, 1972.

SEASONS OF A MARRIAGE
Wright, H. Norman, Ph.D. Ventura, CA: Regal Books,
1982.

STRAIGHT TALK TO MEN AND THEIR WIVES
Dobson, Dr. James C. Waco, TX: Word, Inc., 1980.

THE TAMING OF A TYPE A MALE
Snyder, Chuck. Sisters, OR: Questar, 1989.

TAMING TENSION
Keller, W. Phillip. New York: Vantage Press, 1979.

TENDER WARRIOR
Weber, Stu. Sisters, OR: Multnomah, 1993.

TOO CLOSE TOO SOON
Talley, Jim A. and Bobbie Reed. Nashville: Thomas
Nelson, Inc., 1982.

THE TRAUMA OF TRANSPARENCY
Howard, J. Grant. Portland, OR: Multnomah Press, 1978.

THE WAY THEY LEARN
Tobias, Cindy. Colorado Springs, CO: Focus on the Family
Publishing, 1994.

TURNING HEARTS TOWARD HOME
Zettersten, Rolf, Dallas, TX: Word, Inc., 1992.

YOU CAN PROFIT FROM STRESS
Collins, Gary R., Ph.D. Santa Ana, CA: Vision House
Publishers, 1977.

YOUR FINANCES IN CHANGING TIMES
Burkett, Larry. Chicago, IL: Moody Press, 1982.

WHAT TEENAGERS WISH THEIR PARENTS KNEW
ABOUT KIDS
Ridenour, Fritz. Waco, TX: Word, Inc., 1982.

WHAT WIVES WISH THEIR HUSBANDS KNEW
ABOUT WOMEN.
Dobson, Dr. James C. Wheaton, IL: Tyndale House
Publishers, Inc., 1975.

WHAT'S A SMART WOMAN LIKE YOU DOING
AT HOME
Burton, Linda, Janet Dittmer, and Cheri Loveless. Vienna,
VA: Mother's at Home, 1992.

WHEN GOD DOESN'T MAKE SENSE
Dobson, Dr. James C. Wheaton, IL: Tyndale House
Publishers, Inc., 1993.

WHERE IS GOD WHEN IT HURTS?
Yancey, Philip. Grand Rapids, MI: Zondervan, 1977.

WHY CHILDREN MISBEHAVE
Narramore, Bruce. Grand Rapids, MI: Zondervan, 1980.

YOU'RE SOMEONE SPECIAL
Narramore, Bruce. Grand Rapids, MI: Zondervan, 1978.

Endnotes

Chapter 2

[1]Taylor-Johnson Temperament Analysis® and (T-JTA®) are registered trademarks of Psychological Publications, Inc.

[2]Chuck and Barb Snyder, *Incompatbibility: Grounds for a Great Marriage* (Sisters, Ore.: Questar Publishers, Inc., 1988).

Chapter 6

[1]James Dobson, *What Wives Wish Their Husband Knew About Women* (Wheaton: Tyndale, 1977).

[2]Deborah Tannen, *You Just Don't Understand* (New York: Morrow, 1990).

Chapter 9

[1]Cynthia Ulrich Tobias, *The Way They Learn* (Colorado Springs: Focus on the Family Publishing, 1994).

[2]David Keirsey and Marilyn Bates, *Please Understand Me* (Del Mar, Calif: Prometheus Nemesis, 1978).

[3]Ibid., p. 2.